# Love Letters to Ukraine

*from Uyava*

Любовні листи до України

від Уяви

**RIVER PAW PRESS**

Love Letters to Ukraine from Uyava


First Edition: 2023

ISBN: 978-1-7366871-3-0



Copy Editing English: Kalpna Singh-Chitnis and Candice Louisa Daquin
Copy Editing Ukrainian: Volodymyr Tymchuk and Olena O'Lear

River Paw Press

USA

**www.riverpawpress.com**

# Love Letters to Ukraine

*from Uyava*

Kalpna Singh-Chitnis

With Ukrainian Translation by Volodymyr Tymchuk

Любовні листи до України
від Уяви

Калпна Сінг-Чітніс

Переклав
Володимир Тимчук

**River Paw Press**

# Acknowledgment

A deep bow to Ukraine for giving me its love and trust in abundance, even during a time of immense suffering, caused by the brutal aggression of its enemy nation.

Merci to my eternal friend, Volodymyr Tymchuk. "Love Letters to Ukraine from Uyava," wouldn't have been possible without you.

Deepest gratitude to Dmytro Drozdovskyi at Vsesvit, Sukrita Paul Kumar at Indian Literature, Sahitya Akademi, and Mykhailo Sydorzhevsky at "Ukrayinska literaturna hazeta," for supporting "Love Letters to Ukraine from Uyava," and for publishing its announcement, poetry, translations, and reviews.

Lyudmyla Khersonska, Brian Turner, Ihor Pavliuk, Marianna Cheletska, Anatoliy Anatoliy, Richard Modiano, Yogesh Patel, Michael Whelan, Norm Oppegard, Ami Kaye, Zilka Joseph, Gloria Mindock, Alicia Viguer-Espert and Lyubov Lukina, thanks! You lift me up with your words.

A special thanks to my dear friend, professor Nynke Passi for hosting the magical pre-launch of "Love Letters to Ukraine from Uyava" at the 2023 Soul Bone Literary Festival, and for putting a spotlight on Ukrainian literature.

Olena O'Lear, Candice Louisa Daquin, my soul sisters and poet-friends, you have been my strength. We have moved mountains together. Thanks for your help to me in delivering "Love Letters to Ukraine from Uyava" to the world. No words can thank you enough!

Nirvana and Yuri Botvinkin, gracias for having our back. There are several other names worthy of mention here. Team River Paw Press with the warrior poet and translator of "Love Letters to Ukraine from Uyava," Volodymyr Tymchuk, extend thanks to everyone.

~ *Kalpna Singh-Chitnis*

*A Gift of Love from India to the Land of Skovoroda*

*A Token of Friendship from America to Ukraine*

*A Talisman of Love Songs for the Defenders of Ukraine*

Дар любові землі Сковороди від Індії

Знак дружби Україні від Америки

Любовні пісні як оберіг Захисникам України

# Подяки

Низький уклін Україні за те, що вона щедро обдарувала своєю любов'ю та довірою навіть у час безмірних страждань, спричинених жорстокою агресією ворожої держави.

Спасибі моєму вічному другові Володимирові Тимчуку. «Любовні листи до України від Уяви» були б неможливі без тебе.

Щира подяка Дмитрові Дроздовському з журналу «Всесвіт», Сукріті Паул Кумар з журналу «Індійська література», Сагітья Академі та Михайлові Сидоржевському з «Української літературної газети» за підтримку збірки «Любовні листи до України від Уяви», а також за публікацію її анонсів, вибраних поезій і перекладів та рецензій на неї.

Людмило Херсонська, Браяне Тернере, Ігорю Павлюку, Мар'яно Челецька, Анатолію Анатолію, Річарде Модіано, Йогеше Пателю, Майкле Вілане, Норме Оппеґарде, Емі Кей, Зілко Джозеф, Ґлоріє Міндок, Алісіє Вайґер-Есперт і Любове Лукіна, дякую! Ваші слова мене окрилюють.

Особлива подяка моїй дорогій подрузі професорці Нінке Пассі за організацію чарівної попередньої презентації «Любовних листів до України від Уяви» на літературному фестивалі *Soul Bone 2023,* а також за те, що привернула увагу до української літератури.

Олено О'Лір, Кендіс Луїзо Дакін, мої духовні посестри та подруги-поетеси, ви були моєю силою. Разом ми перевернули гори. Дякую вам за те, що допомогли мені донести до світу «Любовні листи до України від Уяви». Бракує слів, аби висловити всю мою вдячність вам!

Юрію Ботвінкін і Нірвано, дякую вам за підтримку. Є ще кілька імен, які заслуговують на згадку. Команда видавництва *River Paw Press* разом із поетом-воїном і перекладачем «Любовних листів до України від Уяви» Володимиром Тимчуком долучаються до подяки кожному.

~ Калпна Сінг-Чітніс

# CONTENTS

*“A real love letter is made of insight, understanding, and compassion. Otherwise it's not a love letter. A true love letter can produce a transformation in the other person, and therefore in the world. But before it produces a transformation in the other person, it has to produce a transformation within us. Some letters may take the whole of our lifetime to write.” ~ Thich Nhat Hanh*

*“Справжній любовний лист — це плетиво з проникливості, розуміння та співчуття. Інакше це вже не любовний лист. Правдивий любовний лист здатен здійснити перетворення в іншій людині, а відтак і в світі. Але перш ніж він здійснить перетворення в іншій людині, він мусить здійснити перетворення в нас самих.Деякі листи потребують цілого життя, аби бути написаними”. ~ Тхіть Ньят Хань*

# Impressions

## Impassioned Verses of Empathy

Fresh on the heels of editing the wide-ranging and necessary anthology, "Sunflowers: Ukrainian Poetry on War, Resistance, Hope and Peace," poet Kalpna Singh-Chitnis has responded with impassioned verses of empathy in "Love Letters to Ukraine from Uyava," as the war rages on in Ukraine. These poems understand that "there is an urgency to write love poems/ There is an urgency/ to read and listen to poems of love." Singh-Chitnis is a poet whose verses recognize pain, loss, and tenderness. These are poems meant to bridge the divide between one world and another, between a lover and those fighting on the front lines of Ukraine. Throughout these poems, this book implores us: "Let's not close our eyes or look away!" ~ *Brian Turner, Author of "Here, Bullet."*

## A Fierce, Tender, and Passionate Evocation

I am gobsmacked by these poems. A fierce, tender, and passionate evocation of what is at stake in Ukraine and beyond… A truly powerful work. I found myself wishing and wanting more. ~ *Norman M. Oppegard, Sergeant USMC 1968-72*

## The Universe in Letters

How do artists see the world? What do they feel? What meanings do they look for? Who do they address? An artist always asks questions. And they are much more important than answers. Especially when these questions are in letters with boundless love for Ukraine. With indescribable longing and hope. With faith and confidence in victory. Especially when it is talented! Kalpna Singh-Chitnis, the universe in letters. Travel through her universe. Enjoy her words. Look for answers. ~ *Anatoliy Anatoliy (Анатолій Анатолій), Poet, Philologist, and Colonel, participating in the Russian-Ukrainian war*

## Real Windows, Beyond the Nightly News

These are beautifully composed and masterfully crafted poems about life and love in the conflict of Ukraine as experienced by those enduring the war and fighting to defend their country, and about what is happening and happens in the absence of love. These poems are new and very real windows, beyond the nightly news, on the impact of this and any war on the ordinary human condition. They remind us of what is important to the soul when the mind, body, and home are in peril, threatened, and destroyed. They remind us that people far away from the outside, are looking. They can see, feel, hear, and show compassion, empathy and support, and love in many ways, including through poetry. After reading these poems, one questions why this is happening and what is important to live, defend, and even die for? ~ *Michael Whelan, Poet, Military Historian and a Corporal in the Irish Air Corps of Irish Defense Forces, served as a Peacekeeper in South Lebanon and Kosovo.*

## Rhythmic March of Love

We had Auden, and we had Sassoon, but we now have Kalpna Singh-Chitnis with a different take on a war. She unequivocally reminds us that bullets and missiles don't win war, as they can't win our hearts! The Ukrainian warriors are ardently fighting for love. It is their greatest weapon. It is that secret that oozes everywhere in these poems. At the heart, Singh-Chitnis is Buddhist, so it is not surprising that its tranquillity flows unbound here, as in her previous collections, encased in a meditative mien. Instead of the deafening sound of bugles, we are amidst the rhythmic march of love. Singh-Chitnis has created a humane world of remarkable and disturbing stillness, amidst a beast's inhumane war. *~Yogesh Patel MBE - Recipient: Freedom of the City of London*

## Domain of Sanity Amidst the Madness of War

*Love Letters to Ukraine* by Kalpna Singh-Chitnis is an extraordinarily compelling call for love that can transform the insides of both, the writer as well as those who "receive" the letters. Marked by intensity and urgency, the words in these poems acquire a magical power that can make heart to heart connections and create "a survival kit" for people at war. Transcending from the merely personal, the poems evoke an expanse of love and compassion, giving "rise to silence that holds all meaning." Throbbing with life, there is a subtle foreboding of death that can "resurrect truth." To partake of this book of poems is like diving into an ocean of love that hurts but is also soothing and healing. *~ Sukrita Paul Kumar, Poet, Writer and Author of Vanishing Words*

## Essential to the Human Condition: Compassion and Understanding

*Love Letters to Ukraine from Uyava* by Kalpna Singh-Chitnis is a collection of witnesses to suffering, sorrow, and hope, written in a language characterized by clarity and empathy. The emotional horizon that Singh-Chitnis evokes is both expansive and intimate, bringing the reader into contact with what is essential to the human condition: compassion and understanding. *~ Richard Modiano, Author of The Forbidden Lunch Box, and Director Emeritus Beyond Baroque Literary Arts Center*

## Love Poems No One Has Written for Anyone Ever Before...

Love poems addressed not to one's beloved, but to a whole country... A country that resists absolute evil. A country whose glory is proclaimed by people of different nationalities all over the world, united on the side of Good. The name of this country is Ukraine. And it made Kalpna Singh-Chitnis fall in love with it, capturing her imagination ("Uyava" in Ukrainian!) with its will to win and the courage of its defenders. It is from this passionate love that this extraordinary book was born. *~ Olena O'Lear, Ukrainian Poet and Translator*

# A Book of Love, Pure and Overwhelming

The collection of poems, *Love Letters to Ukraine from Uyava*, in the author's metaphor, is a *Survival Kit* for the reader. Those of us who have been traumatized by this war need soothing anointment for our wounds. I am very touched to be one of the addressees of these letters – a very powerful poem named "Defending you." I have to confess, I read the poem with tears in my eyes, so healing and compassionate as it is.

This is a book of love, pure and overwhelming as love should be. This is a book of spirit, strong and willing, as spirit should be.

These days poets write a lot about war and its atrocities, but Kalpna's book struck me with how important it is, to speak love to those who suffer. People are often very lonely in their suffering; they need to be embraced. Kalpna's poetry embraces you. I feel that every single Ukrainian is on her poetical 'mail list.' No one is ignored. She talks to every single person. So inspiring.

*There is a reason why the earth needs*
*the sun, no matter how far the distance.*
*There is no contract between them.*
*God doesn't command their love.*
*Yet, they are there for each other,*
*for the sake of the universe.*

*~ Lyudmyla Khersonska (Людмила Херсонська), Author of "Vse svoi," and "Tyl'naia-litsevaia," reflections on Russian aggression in Ukraine.*

*February 10th, 2023*
*Odesa, Ukraine*

## Fiercely Passionate and Compassionate

Kalpna Singh-Chitnis's new collection, "Love Letters to Ukraine from Uyava" is fiercely passionate and compassionate. Through her "love letters," Singh-Chitnis conducts a symphony of love set to the cacophony of war machines. Her letters are deeply felt evocations; human stories live in their lines. Their immediacy underscores how relentlessly war touches everything - the land, its people, even the animals. Kalpna Singh-Chitnis's book is a testament to human connectedness, the need for a deep and meaningful anchor during times of tragedy, trauma, and stress, and the power of love through the infernal blast of bombs and missiles, *"No one should die without love. No one should live in its absence." ~ Ami Kaye, Publisher & Editor, Glass Lyre Press, LLC*

## A Declaration of the Victory of the Ukrainian and the Human Spirit

This book is an outpouring of passionate words, an appeal to the heart in times of war and in the very face of death. It is a love song to Ukraine and its people, in particular the soldiers and those on the forefront of the war. Often through the persona of Uyava—which means imagination in Ukrainian, Singh-Chitnis takes risks, assumes different identities and characters, and sometimes renders short film-like pieces that reflect her background in filmmaking. Her poems can be personal or reach out into history, referencing the Vietnam War, or the horrors of the partition of India and Pakistan, and they can range from the dramatic and declamatory to the philosophic and more understated. The focus is always Ukraine, the determination of its brave people. "If there is another day, another life, /I promise to rise like a Phoenix/from the ashes of my being/in your skies, blue and yellow." These are not just poems of love but an exhortation to fight on, a declaration of the victory of the Ukrainian and the human spirit. ~ *Zilka Joseph, Author of In Our Beautiful Bones, Sparrows and Dust, Sharp Blue Search of Flame*

## This Book Gives Meaning to What is Needed

As the tragic invasion continues in Ukraine with millions displaced and many dying, in *Love Letters to Ukraine from Uyava*, the poet reminds the world, "No one should live without love,/No one should live in its absence." Her love letters are passionate and beautifully written. They are "the most essential item to carry in your pack/when you are headed for war." This book gives meaning to what is needed as Ukraine fights for freedom. Kalpna Singh-Chitnis speaks of her ancestors surviving war, and just like them, Ukrainians will testify, so history is accurate. *~Gloria Mindock, Editor of Červená Barva Press, Author of Award-Winning ASH*

## Everyone Has Their Own Vocation

Volodymyr's works and translations are insightful, truthful, sensual, and frank, which I, as a composer, transform into musical reproductions and try to convey semantic and figurative associations through the word to create my own vision. Kalpna Singh-Chitnis' translated poems have an impact, they stir the soul. So it is not surprising that an eternally difficult range of feelings interferes while working on them." ~ *Lyubov Lukina, Methodology Teacher, Pianist, and Composer*

## The Yellow-Blue of the Indian Mystical Book of Poems

The elements of Love and Freedom are fundamental, universal, spiritual, and poetical, which always unite people. Today, when the destiny of humanity is being determined in Ukraine, it is significant that the lieutenant colonel of the heroic Armed Forces of Ukraine, poet Volodymyr Tymchuk, whom I personally know and have been reading for a long time, has translated the yellow and blue (colors of the Ukrainian flag), mystical Indian book of poetry "Love Letters to Ukraine from Uyava" by the wonderful Indian-American poet Kalpna Singh- Chitnis, published as a Ukrainian-English bilingual collection of poems by the American publishing house "River Paw Press."

This is co-creating a new value and cultural reality. As a result bringing us closer to peace, victory, and good on earth, with a projection of eternity and infinity of human souls in a multicolored, unifying, and life-giving pulsating rhythm, where the courses of every string are different, but the one beautiful path of humanity that leads to the creator.

Let's look at this exotic, organic book with poem like:

*"I have followed your light to come home./ But I do not know where I come from, / what's my name. / Dear Ukraine, you can call me—Uyava!"*

*to see how a common spiritual child, a representative of the Indian and Ukrainian people, will bring us all closer to purification by a drop, a spark, and a metaphor...*

*~ Ihor Pavliuk, Writer, Translator, Scholar, Doctor of Social Communications, People's Poet of Ukraine, Winner of the British PEN Prize and Swiss Literary Prize 2021.*

## A Courier of Love, a Healer, a Priest, a Lover

Kalpna Singh-Chitnis breathes love into her latest poetry collection, *Love Letters to Ukraine from Uyava.* With threads of prayers, compassion, courage, and poetry, she weaves a beautiful tapestry for Ukraine. She will even make love to the devil to distract him from conjuring more carnage. Though poetry and love do not guarantee the warriors return home, she understands the importance of carrying the essence of the land in their pockets, sunflowers, and love poems, which she provides. She talks to Ukraine from the wisdom of one soul to another, cognizant that answers are not given, only questions; she recognizes the power of fear, "one mistake and everything is finished," she whispers, referring to land mines.

Kalpna never shies away from the horrors, cruelties, and wounds inflicted by war but uses her innate lyricism, and compassion for Nature's creatures, to portray the terrible and beautiful, while planting seeds of hope, transformation, and even joy. Her cross-cultural life experience provides us with a sample of the ideal marriage between India's spirituality and America's practicality. Buddhist training and practices inspire her to become a courier of love, a healer, a priest, a lover, reminding us over and over that Love is the glue binding the universe. Whether invoking The Invincible Durga, the purity of the lotus flower, the sound of the conch shell calling us to action, or how to sit in silence under the Bodhi Tree of our individual consciousness, she's always present for the beloved-warrior. At the same time, she's mindful of the Christian background of Ukrainians and not only treats the icons of their spiritual traditions with respect but uses them to connect with her beloved and ground her poems. Her filmography career informs her poetry with hypnotic images and music. Sometimes her clear, direct language reminds us of Rumi. "Cut down your shackles," she encourages the Spirit of Ukraine, and the intense longing and pain of separation in "Saffron Love," evokes Jelaludin's "Song of the Reed."

Nevertheless, the power of Kalpna's poetic voice springs from her deep feelings of compassion and sense of beauty which are as unique as each sunflower. You'll be inspired to meditate on these poems over and over.

*~ Alicia Viguer-Espert is the Author of Holding a Hummingbird*

## Love Letters to Ukraine, as an Exemplar of Love Poems

The love that arises from the shape of fire evolves into an intimate, authentic note. The poet experiences Ukraine not just with her imagination but with every inch of her body and soul. That is why her feelings, mixed with grief and indignation, emerge as a poem that travels the world and returns home each passing day. This is not just a course of poetry—it is a way of KNOWING—through touches, sounds, and colors, dipping each finger and measuring the depth of the image hidden behind the map that outlines Ukraine's physical and spiritual spaces.

Thoughts break "Ominous Silence" and "Air Raid Sirens" skillfully, fulfilling their ritualistic mission, like a mantra from Buddhist scriptures. These thoughts carry a unique evangelizing energy of creation metaphorically personified in poems by the heavenly flower *Udumbara.*

Living through the days of the terrible 2022 with the full-scale invasion of Ukraine by the Russian troops in precise temporal images and spatially recognizable locations, the author writes not just a poetic wartime diary but a special Psalm of faith:

*I hear the words you do not say, / write them in my notebook / and listen to them, like Psalms.*

Thus, the image of the Phoenix is the most evident, convincing, and faithful way for her to communicate with Ukraine from across the ocean:

*If there is another day, another life, / I promise to rise like a Phoenix / from the ashes of my being / in your skies, blue and yellow.*

Kalpna Singh-Chitnis' patriotic poems are her original interpretation of love poetry, which grows from nostalgic listening to the voices of Ukraine, attempting to go beyond the pathos and rhetorics of textbook ideas, expanding horizons with visions, overcoming fears and deep wounds with one word—LOVE.

~ *Marianna Cheletska, Literary Critic*

## From Heaven and Earth

*~ Introducing "Love Letters to Ukraine from Uyava" and the "One" who carried it in his pocket to deliver to his nation*

We have our plans, but the universe has plans of its own for us. What we do (knowingly and unknowingly) are our actions (*Karma*), but the results of these actions, often not in our control, are our destiny (*Prarabdh*). "Love Letters to Ukraine from Uyava," was planned by the universe. It was destined to be written and translated simultaneously into two languages, by two writers from two different worlds, with the same passion and love for Ukraine.

You go out to heal the world, and in return, you are healed yourself. You want to give to the universe, instead, you receive a cornucopia of blessings for yourself. What is more profound is that you extend your helping hand to others, and in return, your own soul is rescued. I must mention that the process of writing "Love Letters to Ukraine from Uyava" has touched me with such profoundness I had not experienced before. Every poem in this book, an offering to the earth of Ukraine, has brought me enormous healing and helped me cope with my own loss of someone who twice served in the Iraq war. Who incarnated in the spirits of the soldiers of Ukraine, ready to make ultimate sacrifices for their country and willing to embrace anyone standing with them with open arms. Such blessings do not shower from heaven at a time when drones strike and fire rains in a promised land where you miraculously arrive crossing oceans and borders, without any ship, train, or airplane, without any visa or passport, walking effortlessly through every wall, crossing all barrier seen and unseen like Quantum Physics explains. Even our own will is unable to stop us from being there when a will stronger than our own takes us in a direction we are meant to go. As if we are summoned to fulfill a destiny, and in my case, it was to write love poems at someone's invitation for those who fiercely stood in the face of their enemy to protect their country, and bring victory and glory to their land, resulting in me writing *Love Letters to Ukraine from Uyava.*

When wars happen, devils roam the planet in their dance shoes, and angels sing tenderly in the hearts of those who love and are ready to make any sacrifice to save the world. In such a time and place, finding a translator for your poems is something beyond imagination, even for poets. But it did happen. I was fortunate to encounter the greatest admirer of my poetry on the battlefields of Ukraine. Someone who was meant to be the reader and bearer of my love poems for his people and country in his language in a most profound way. It was heartening to learn that the very warrior who manifested from the deepest realm of the universal consciousness was already leading my cultural mission of publishing "Sunflowers: Ukrainian Poetry on War Resistance, Hope and Peace," an anthology I curated and edited in October 2022, to amplify the voices of Ukrainian writers, and help Ukrainian causes, in his country. He was one of the poets in the book. After the launch of "Sunflowers," all the writers and translators had left, but someone stayed to say thanks and help me clean up after the party. Today it's my great honor and privilege to introduce that very special someone, a prolific poet and one of the finest warriors of Ukraine, Volodymyr Tymchuk, to our readers.

Volodymyr Tymchuk, a poet, writer, and a lieutenant colonel in the Ukrainian Armed Forces, is the translator of "Love Letter to Ukraine from Uyava," River Paw Press (2023). I must acknowledge I couldn't possibly have found a better translator for my poems than him. Tymchuk, who began his literary career with his debut poetry collection «Vesniani kolovoroty» ("Spring Whirlpools"), published in (2009), performed by Yevhen Vakhniak State Honored Chapel of Ukraine, «Boyan», has published over a dozen collections of poetry, poetry anthologies and books of prose in the Ukrainian language. His first collection of poems also published some of his translations from Slavic languages, featuring poems by the President of the Chechen Republic of Ichkeria, Zelimkhan Yandarbiyev. His second collection of short stories and essays, «Slovodiem» (Word-Acted), was published in 2014. In 2015, on the anniversary of the deportation of Crimean Tatars by Russia (Soviet "Union" at that time) commemorated the victims of the deportation to remind the world that occupiers and their collaborators were still committing crimes against humanity in the annexed Autonomous Republic of Crimea and the city of Sevastopol, and the idea of the art project "Bakhchysarai. 2021" was born in Lviv. Volodymyr Tymchuk and authors like S. Kokche, Maye Safet, six translators, and four artists prepared a unique edition of the first bilingual book written in the Ukrainian and Crimean Tatar languages in three months, which was presented with a question "*Do we, the authors, expect a presentation in the liberated Ukrainian Bakhchysarai in six years?*"

In 2017 Volodymyr Tymchuk created another significant project called "Ukraine and Lithuania: At the Crossroads of Histories and Values" based on the postcards by Vidmantas Kudarauskas from Lithuania for the parallel placement and comparisons of the historical events of two ancient European nations who valued freedom in their expressions. He also prepared "Verlaine and the Song" (2017) and "Opus Khody" № 2399" (March Opus) (2018) with his Lithuanian friend Juozas Valiušaitis in just 69 hours and 21 minutes, which was submitted to the Guinness Book of World Records for creating the fastest book from concept to completion. Between 2018 and 2022, he worked on writing, translating, editing, and publishing several literary projects, such as the translations of war poems of the 1st World war poets from English, German, Hungarian; the translations of Christmas poems from Byelorussian, Latvian, Italian, Portugal, and other cultures, and the key anthology «In principio erat Verbum: Ukrainian poems of war» about first 100 days of Life from February 24, 2022, in Ukrainian and French. During this period, he also authored: «The B.a:S-i)l's #light» (2018), «Vidchuty misto stopoyu (z Toboyu)» (2019), «In Angels' Order» (2019), «East … Sunrise» (2020), «Azov … Crossed» (2020), «From Cossack Hetmanate's Infinity» (2021). He was awarded the "Bohdan Khmelnytskyi Prize" for the best coverage of military themes in literature and art (2016), the "Markiyan Shashkevych Poetic Nomination for Lviv Regional Cultural Prize" (2020), and "Volyanik-Shwabinskyi Literary and Scientific Award" (2022).

A fascinating part of my acquaintance and collaboration with the translator of "Love Letters to Ukraine from Uyava," was discovering the poet in him. Volodymyr Tymchuk is a brilliantly sensitive, fiercely patriotic, hopelessly romantic, and deeply knowledgeable poet of Ukraine whose core is as bright and tender as the white flesh of a coconut bathed in sweet fragrant water, hidden under the layers of its coarse fibers and hardened shell. This discovery reassured me, that no one could understand my poetry better than him, to translate them into his language. From the onset, there was no doubt that the universe had made our connection in order to work on this important task; to write and translate a book of poetry on love no foreign poet had written for Ukraine before. There was no ambiguity between the poet and translator. Our conversations were informal and easy flowing, like two friends meeting and catching up with each other after many years. How such familiarity between us was born has remained a mystery for us both. There were some revelations and confessions in our conversations. And one of them, was that the translator sent from heaven, was once envious of my poet and her cultural mission in Ukraine. *How could someone from a foreign land with a foreign tongue walk in on the literary stage of his beloved country, to do what he was meant to do for his folks?* Hearing these words coming from a decorated soldier and a celebrated poet of Ukraine, was flattering. Thus, I held no malice against the soldier-poet.

Volodymyr appeared intrigued by my background of working with the soldiers of the United States Army and Marine Corps officers for making my debut feature film “Goodbye My Friend” (2011), in Hollywood, against the backdrop of the Iraq war. My attention to international politics and warfare (due to my background in teaching International Relations at the university level in India) appealed to him. He watched my feature film to know me as an artist and a professional. The exchanges of our ideas, visions, and views on religion, philosophy, spirituality, art, culture, politics, and war, resulted in us learning more and more about one other. His experiences as a soldier, a poet, a family man, and a cultural ambassador of his country, were exceptional.

He carried out military tasks during his missions on the eastern Ukrainian front (2014–2021) and acutely pointed to the severity of events that were taking place during that time, by recording his emotions, impressions, and thoughts directly from the battlefield; asking a question—*"When is it possible to live in harmony with yourself, if not every moment?"* "Being in the Moment " was important for both poet and translator, one a ZSU warrior and the other, a Buddha's warrior. The poet's response to his own question, resulted in him writing three, four, and five... poetry collections, yet to be published. But somehow, I managed to read some of his poems written during that time (without his knowledge) and surprised him, by translating them into English and publishing them in some American journals.

Volodymyr Tymchuk's poems are born of the conflicts between the two worlds he belongs to. The world he passionately loves stays — in harmony with him, and the world that challenges his views and establishes the fact that conflict is a constant phenomenon, therefore, it is unavoidable, and love, peace, and freedom are fragile; thus, they must be coveted and protected. In one of his noted poems, ‘The Spirit of the Eternal Element,’ he writes, *"I feel intoxicated, standing between the two worlds protecting, loving, and living."* The very juxtaposition and contrast of a warrior poet's outlook toward life and love drew my attention to study and translate more of his poems burning with passion, cosmic energy, and patriotic fervor, that we may have the chance to read in his soon to be published poetry collection, “Ukraine: The Healing Word.”

As a translator, I discovered that Volodymyr Tymchuk is not an easy poet to translate. His verses are multilayered and must be understood in their proper contexts, which is a key to the poet's heart and his world of poetry. Volodymyr appreciated my efforts to translate his poems into English and publish them but gently conveyed that he doesn't write just to get his works published. His works have *missions*. And one of his such missions carried out by him was his latest project, "In principio erat Verbum. Ukraine. Poetry of War," a bilingual anthology of 100 poems on the first 100 days of the war in French, Italian, German, and other languages. So, as poets, we stood on the same ground with our missions, and he knew this.

Working with Volodymyr for eight weeks, almost every day for a few hours in real time, to write, share and translate the poems of "Love Letters to Ukraine from Uyava," allowed me to know him, not only as a poet and translator, but also as a person and a serviceman. While being with me on Zoom, as a writer and the translator of my poems, he was also a father, helping his son do his homework, side by side, trying to find the best TV show for him to watch, while we discussed and translated the poems of "Love Letters to Ukraine from Uyava." At times, he was just another Ukrainian who would celebrate Christmas in his traditional outfit and joyously share how satisfied he was after eating *Kutia,* a traditional Christmas dish, with his family. In the mornings, I would watch him chew on dry bread and apple slices with coffee for breakfast, with his eyes glued to the screen, to finish one last translation of the day before heading to the Hetman Petro Sahaidachnyi National Ground Forces Academy in Lviv, where he taught. During his busy schedule, some of our conversations would take place on Messenger, giving me the opportunity to virtually travel in the palms of his hands, watching sunshine and the snow falling in Lviv, listening to the air raid sirens, learning about the military drill being interrupted, sheltering until the missiles are shot down, and the threat is over. On such a day, he would translate my poems on his phone to help me meet the deadlines of submitting them to Ukrainian magazines, which thoughtfully invited my poems. He would take pride in introducing me and my poetry at literary events in Ukraine and talking about our anthology "Sunflowers: Ukrainian Poetry on War Resistance, Hope and Peace" at museums, libraries, and other significant venues internationally. But then, there were times when I lose contact with him entirely, for days, and our common friend, Olena O'Lear in Kyiv, would help me find him. Also, whenever the poet and translator disagreed on a particular matter, which rarely happened, Olena would play referee at the invitation of Volodymyr, who trusted her more than myself for *practical Ukrainian wisdom* and the translations of his rhythmic poems. Which was all 'cool' with me, as Americans say, when we feel enlightened.

Ukraine blessed me with many great friends. Some of them, for high-security reasons, could only communicate via poetry they would write and share from the battlefields. Through them, I had exposure to the everyday life of Ukrainians and the warriors of Ukraine during intense times of conflict, which helped me write *letters to Ukraine* with authenticity, urgency, sincerity, and nearly the same passion Ukrainians might do. Sometimes, I would share the special war coverage in Ukraine from American media with my Ukrainian friends. Volodymyr would read, watch and reflect upon them with deep interest. When Soledar fell, he shared his poem on the salt city of Ukraine, and his other war poems, which allowed me to look deeply into the heart of a real soldier. On December 22, 2022, I sent him the special report of the New York Times,

"Caught on Camera, Traced by Phone: The Russian Military Unit That Killed Dozens in Bucha," and he wrote back — *The death of every civilian and his knights will be avenged.* Amidst all that was happening and still happening in Ukraine, it has brought the world a new awakening, reminding us that the most important things to die for, are love and freedom. And we shared these aspirations for Ukraine and humanity in our conversations every time.

In my literary career, spanned over more than three decades, I wrote and published several books in both my languages (Hindi and English) in both my countries (India and USA). I also collaborated with many poets and translators across the globe, but hardly came across anyone working with such passion and efficiency as Volodymyr did. His deep insight into my poetry, made the translation of "Love Letters to Ukraine from Uyava" almost effortless. I hardly ever had to explain my poems to him, yet he always delivered their accurate translations. Volodymyr would read the cultural references in my poems with great interest and often surprised me with his extensive research on them. He kept up with me at all levels of creativity, and I did the same.

In many ways, we both were alike; hard-working, passion-driven individuals with excellent work ethics and daydreamers like no other. Seeing my love for his country, helping Ukrainian causes, promoting Ukrainian literature, and empathy for his people earned his trust in me. One day when he was in a great mood, he told me, *You will make the best ambassador for Ukraine in India and the USA.* And looking at his love and pride for his country and his dedication to his motherland, I told him, that *someday, he would make a great President of Ukraine,* our conversation ended in laughter.

The hardest part of this heartening saga was the production of "Love Letters to Ukraine from Uyava." After working on the book day and night for eight weeks, we both were burnt out. Volodymyr had to leave, and I was left with all the logistical responsibilities of editing, publishing, and promoting yet another bilingual book on the world stage soon after publishing "Sunflowers: Ukrainian Poetry on War, Resistance, Hope and Peace" in less than four months. The changing dynamics of the war take a toll on all aspects of the life of everyone involved in it. It often takes away the joy of doing things that are beautiful and meaningful. Hurts are deeper than poetry can fathom, and several love letters to Ukraine were not meant to be delivered. From the depths of despair, as an American, I had to remind myself of our commitments to Ukraine and my pledges to its cultural resistance. Sometimes holding Yellow and Blue all alone, but never without hope. *From Artilleries to Love Poems, to Tanks to Wings of Freedom...* America's promises to Ukraine must be kept, and India's sacred gift of love poems for Ukraine must be delivered with respect. It has been a great privilege to pen and publish "Love Letters to Ukraine from Uyava" to reach those it has been written for. My joy on fulfilling this task is infinite, and my heart is filled with gratitude.

May these letters create bridges in our readers' hearts to connect with Ukraine and allow the world to see its heart longing for love, peace, and freedom. Glory and victory to the defenders of Ukraine! Slava Ukraine!

Kalpna Singh-Chitnis

February 24, 2023, Greater Los Angeles, CA, USA

# Foreword

What does it take for one from a quite different culture and background, to reach across time and space and share empathy and kindness with another? It is often said this is the purpose of poetry and I would agree. Bearing this in mind, then no wonder *Love Letters to Ukraine from Uyava* by Kalpna Singh-Chitnis, touched me profoundly.

As a reader of poetry, we delve into poems blind and seek their truth. But what of the poet? In *Love Letters to Ukraine from Uyava,* well established literary figure Kalpna Singh-Chitnis, pours her soul into these gifts for Ukraine, with the same urgent sincerity she employed when putting together the Ukraine anthology S*unflowers: Ukrainian Poetry on War, Resistance Hope and Peace* (River Paw Press) just as she did with the anthology; *Parables of the Pandemic* whilst we were all in the throes of Covid-19.

Singh-Chitnis who has flourished as a poet, writer, teacher, actor and film director, is also the Editor-in-Chief of *Life and Legends* and Translation Editor of *IHRAF Literary* in New York. Her multifaceted creativity is both impossible and very real, she is wedded to the creative world and despite being prodigiously busy, carves out time to support others in rare and unexpected ways. Her generosity is both sincere and unending, Singh-Chitnis doesn't seek acclaim so much as possessing a true humanitarian spirit, which is evoked through her numerous projects supporting worthy and timely causes. Such honest empathy while rare, is at the heart of her ability to write and reach others.

In *Love Letters to Ukraine from Uyava*, Singh-Chitnis compiles a series of echo refrain poems for an embattled nation. Her own sympathy is not sentimental so much as pragmatic and hopeful, she doesn't just write, she acts.

*Knowing I dipped my toe in a stream / not knowing it was a sea. (Knowing).*

Her own Buddhist learnings, her active participation in spiritual practice and engaging the natural world, flourishes in her writing and own life. Some say, you cannot separate a creative from their work and I would agree. Singh-Chitnis spellbinds her readers with her reality, reflected back to us in a lesson. This is not a patronizing tone, but a welcoming one. Join her, think on these things, help others, be more. It is both an antithesis to the 'me, me, me' modern culture, and a meditation on what matters most.

*There is no glory in a war./ Every home has a shrine./A war cannot be defined. /It can only be lived or imagined.* (War: A One Way Street).

In Singh-Chitnis's poem Nothing Is Permanent, she considers what mortality is, how we cease and yet continue, and what part humanity plays in the creation and endurance of the world. These deeply philosophical considerations, are presented simply, without pretense, and open within us, a desire to think beyond the moment, to quell our penchant for laziness and try to reach greater heights when it comes to our world. We are after all, not alone, and each of us are linked, therefore we owe a debt of gratitude and allegiance to those who struggle, hence the necessity and value of poetry collections in times of war — a long established tradition, because whom better to speak on war but the poet?

*Let's not cast doubts about / why I am here. Who am I? / I am here at your invitation. / We are in this hell together! / Searching for our paradise lost* (Paradise Lost).

This could be interpreted as a self-fulfilling need to insert oneself into another's suffering, but the purpose is quite the opposite. When a poet engages with a cause, and feels for its people, then the necessity of comparison is not narcissistic but a way of challenging us all to consider beyond ourselves. Often the best way of achieving this is by demonstration of similarity. We know joy from experience and from the contrast of grief. We know others pain by our own. It's humility at its purest when we seek to witness others pain by recalling our own struggles. In this, we are united, we go through life together rather than separately.

*Like a princess of an era gone by, I write songs, / like long shadows cast on the dunes by the evening sun, / and ask the winds to deliver my messages to you / on your battlefields.* (Saffron Love).

We talk of empathy often, but how many of us rise up from our armchair and palpably try to engage and produce manifest change? Singh-Chitnis is one such social justice warrior, with her legion of creative directions, her purpose outgrows the ordinary and becomes extraordinary. She is not mere empath but directly doing battle for others to see inequity and injustice and act. Her words are as much battle cries as they are truths, and she implores the reader to become radically engaged in change. Again, isn't this the crux of poetry and shouldn't more of us be able to write outside of our own musings, and infect the hearts of others with a call to action?

*Since when has the sun begun to rise / in the night sky of California? / Good morning, dear soldier! / Do you see the moon rising / in the morning sky of Kharkiv?* (The One Who Loves).

Singh-Chitnis unites far flung countries together, able to paint our simple human similarities rather than focus on our differences. So often we consider wars, 'other' countries problems, without seeing the universality of war, and its ultimate destruction of us all. Rather than becoming stuck on tragedy or futility of war, Singh-Chitnis brings vignettes of experiences together, so we feel as we read her poetry, that we are living moments and in so doing, understanding at a deeper level.

*There was no Christmas in your trenches, dear Ukraine. / Santa wore camouflage and gave his robe back to God in protest. /There was no celebration of the new year / in your snowfields dotted with blood./ But we have another day of sunshine, / the saplings of hope in our roots, and flower buds / in the branches of our bones waiting for spring.* (The New Year's Eve).

Is it trite for a non-soldier living in California to write of Ukraine? Or is this the reflective skill of poetry, whereby differences become mirrors, and similarities, reflections upon water. Where we grow as we read, through the intentionality of the author to proffer truths that all of us can relate to. When one has the willingness, and sacrifice to ask disparate others, what can I do to help? And part of that need, is to illustrate the irrationality and curse of war, whilst remaining hopeful of its cessation? Whilst I may be a huge confessional poetry fan, I am deeply moved and appreciative of the energies and necessity of raising awareness, beyond the sound-bite of nightly news coverage. In so doing, Singh-Chitnis has conjured up the real people of Ukraine. We see them.

In the poem *Soledar*, Singh-Chitnis breathes hope into the wreckage of war, by her simple reminder that when we are physically torn down, our roots remain, and as long as those fundamentals stand, we are not lost:

*There may not be any walls left standing in your city, / but you have your foundations, the fundamentals, / the grounds you stand on in your offensive.*

In *A Year of the War*, Singh-Chitnis, describes what we can all palpably immediately recognize, the trauma of losing what we took for granted, and being in an incomplete state of fragmentation:

*It has been a year of the war. / We have lost the concept of time. / We have adjusted our body clock / and turned around the seasons in our minds / to live—not merely survive.*

The tension of words, its relentless pace, the specificity of language and gentle hope, make this a tremendous poem of compassion, understanding and unity. We take away from these words, a reminder that we endure, we can be more than merely surviving, we can truly live. It may seem ill timed, given the continuum of the war, but it's exactly what is needed in dark times. That light, that reminder of our capacity to rebuild. One of my favorite poems *War And Flowers*, evoked this most palpably in these searing lines—

*They did not go to the temples, churches and synagogues, / or offer themselves to God and Godmen. / They went to honor the coffins of the soldiers / and unmarked graves of the braves and innocents.*

And the final line in the poem; everyone takes a new role in a war. The simplicity of this belies the wisdom and raw guts of war. We will never stop having wars, as much as many of us wish we could. But without outrage and truth, war might continue to be glamorized or seen as a necessary part of the human condition which is really the greatest lie of all. Yet with its enduring reality, one must understand the roles in war, whether we approve or not. And *t*he anguish of those roles, so often smothered by spectacle, becomes its real legacy. For without those brave souls, even greater atrocities might exist, and justice would be a lost dream.

Fortunately, Singh-Chitnis bequeaths us such wisdom, in a life of myriad experiences, her own proximity to conflict unforgotten, sings most palpably:

*The last time I heard an air raid siren, I was five. / Eating dinner in my courtyard, I had to leave my plate / for the moon. The lights went off.* (War at Five).

The poet's evocation of such terrors, speaks to greater universal terrors, our collective grief and horror as well as the simple juxtaposition of physical things versus spiritual. In my mind's eye, the five-year-old is evoked, her left behind plate, as the world went dark. If we know one thing it is, that war vanquishes peace and peace is what our hearts seek. Why then do wars keep happening? If we do not keep asking that, perhaps they'll continue as tapestries in the legacy of humanity, and not a something to seek an end to.

*Instead, it is to accept what we have been deprived of / with utmost dignity, only to have the aspiration for / the freedom we must have and to make / all that is denied possible for us.* (Dear Ukraine, Happy Christmas!).

What I particularly cherished in this collection, was the adroit method of combining an appreciation and empathy for a foreign country, alongside Singh-Chitnis's own heritage and country of origin (India). Perhaps only a polyglot, having lived in multiple countries, with the intentional wisdom of such multiculturalism, can pen such solace.

*A river has a destiny of its own. It can wash off the sins of anyone. (The Sand in Our Eyes).*

With translation of all poems into Ukrainian, these poems speak on multiple levels. Aside the social conscience, this collection is the refrain from a broken heart. The testimony between two war-torn lovers, the nimble language of loss and reconciliation and pain.

When she writes, she's splitting her heart as well as her mercy for another nation, and combining that heartache, reflecting her own experiences of war and suffering, she holds the two like a bloody reminder of its futility and agonies in *Promise*:

*Every soldier has a poet / hidden in his heart,/ often killed in friendly fire.*

I've yet to work out how Singh-Chitnis has the time and energies for all that she does, other than her being a whirlwind of well-intentioned actions, which more of us should strive to be. In addition to a prodigious output as a writer, Singh-Chitnis holds a degree in Film Directing from the New York Film Academy and works as an independent filmmaker in Hollywood. Despite this lofty success, her writing reflects the humility she has toward planet earth, and she doesn't subscribe to the materialism of the world so much as its beautiful heart. Empathy and deeper understanding aren't learned in a school room, they are absorbed and shared through raw truth and suffering:

*We are sick of telling the world, / how to spell our names correctly!" "Vladimir is Russian, and Volodymyr is Ukrainian, / Do you get it?* (Misspelling).

Having the fortune to have read all of Kalpna Singh-Chitnis's creative work thus far, I am palpably looking forward to her next collection, *Trespassing My Ancestral Land* forthcoming from *Finishing Line Press*. Is it any wonder her work has been translated into Spanish, French, Italian, German, Portuguese, Albanian, Czech, Arabic, Nepali, Urdu, Bengali, Telugu, Malayalam, Gujarati and now Ukrainian? Her universalism is the core of her ability to reach others. It is my sincere belief that such social warriors lend us the language and determining to believe individuals can have a hand in change. This is surely, the heart of poetry, and why poets such as Chitnis are so utterly necessary, in war time, and in peace.

~ *Candice Louisa Daquin, Senior Editor Indie Blu(e) Publishing.*

"Love Letters to Ukraine from Uyava" is among the most important books of American, Ukrainian, and Indian literary societies with a cultural mission."

*Volodymyr Tymchuk*
*(Poet, Translator, and Lieutenant Colonel of the Armed Forces of Ukraine)*

«Любовні листи до України від Уяви» — одна з найважливіших книг для американської, української та індійської літературних спільнот, книга, яка має культурну місію».

*Володимир Тимчук*
*(Поет, перекладач, підполковник Збройних сил України)*

## The Heart of Ukraine

Dear Sweet Land,
you do not know about the letters
someone is writing for you.

But worry not, they won't set the world on fire.
Just care for your dear heart
soon to be stolen.

# Серце України

Дорога мила земле,
про листи, що їх тобі пишуть,
не знаєш нічого.

Та не зважай! Через них світ не кинеться в полум'я.
Це тільки турбота про серце твоє дороге,
небавом украдене.

# A Warrior Wants to Read Love Poems

Why would a warrior like to read love poems?
Shouldn't he be reading poetry on war cries,
words of anger, torment, hatred, and vengeance?
But no, he wants to read love poems, and I wonder why?

Maybe because he wants to feel warm?
Hunkered down, plowing through snowfields,
he defends his borders from a beast who has brought
ill omens to his land, where the horizon blurs
in blinding light of the sun, and one crosses over
to another shore, like a crane forced to migrate from
its native land, in the grip of cruel, bloody Winter.

A warrior wants to read love poems.
But I have stopped writing love poems
waiting for our warriors to return,
year after year, from one season to another,
eager to hear their footfalls,
their knocks at our doors.
Somewhere, I have given up.
Somewhere I have given up hope for love.
As love and poetry do not guarantee
the return of our warriors. I have tried all.
The storms in the desert swallow them.
They are swept in the gorges of the Himalayas,
absorbed into the earth like snow melting
from the eyes of Ukraine. But not in vain.

A warrior wants to read love poems.
He wants to carry them in his pockets like seeds of sunflowers,
chew on them when famished, and share them with his brothers,
who have no one to write love poems for them.
He wants to sprinkle them in *chornozem,
stained with the blood and tears of his nation,
with the hope that love will grow when conflict is over.
But the nib of my pen is broken, and there is no ink left in my inkpot.

A warrior wants to read love poems, never written before.
I sharpen my pencil in a hurry before he goes.
I scribble something on his chest, where his name appears,
where his dog tag sits like the armor on his chest.
No, you can't read my words. They are camouflaged.

Love poems aren't for everyone. They must be protected
from the eyes of tyrants and dictators—no matter what the cost.

**Chornozem — Black soil found in the Eurasian steppes and countries such as Ukraine, Russia, Romania, and others.*

## А воїн хоче любові вірші читати

Що воїна тут спонукає читати любові вірші?
Не краще хіба прочитати про скрики війни,
про ненависть і про страждання, про гнів і про помсту?
Натомість він хоче читати любові вірші. Цікаво, чому?

Можливо тому, що він прагне відчути тепло.
Пригнувшись постійно в засипаних снігом полях,
боронить кордони від звіра, що в край свій приніс
зла знаки, у нім розпливається обрій
у сонячнім сяйві, хтось змінює змушено берег
на інший, як той журавель, що мігрує з місць рідних
в полоні зими, скривавленої і цілковито жорстокої.

А воїн хоче любові вірші читати.
Та я припинила писати любові вірші
в чеканні на воїнів наших повернення,
за роком рік, від пори до пори,
у прагненні чути їх кроки,
їх стукіт у двері.
Здалася подекуди я.
І втратила я на кохання надію —
Кохання і вірші не гарантують
повернення воїнів наших. Я спробувала.
Їх поглинають бурі в пустелі.
Несуться вони в Гімалаїв ущелинах,
землею вбираючись, снігу подібно,
що тане з очей України. Проте не дарма.

А воїн хоче любові вірші читати.
Він хоче їх мати в кишенях, мов соняху зерня,
щоб лузати, голод обманюючи, і з братами ділитися,
із тими, яким ці вірші любові не пише ніхто.
Він хоче просякнути їх чорноземом,
що кров'ю й сльозами народу политим,
з надією, що, як конфлікти закінчать, любов все зростатиме.
…Проте ось зламалося в мене перо. Чорнило в чорнильниці теж
закінчилося.

А воїн бажає читати вірші любові, які ще ніхто не писав.
У поспіху, поки не зник він, я гострю олівчик.
Виводжу на грудях його, де ім'я,
де гордо заслужене носить звання,

де місце жетону поверх броні, невідомі слова —
Ви їх прочитати не здатні. Вони — замасковані все ж.
Бо вірші любові — вони не для всіх. Їх слід захищати
від ока тирана, від ока диктатора — байдуже, якою — ціна.

## Poems of Love For Ukraine

Dear Ukraine, I will write you poems of love
no one has written before for anyone.

They would be marvels among the wonders of
the world. A world that questions everything
but provides us with no real answers.

But I shall keep my promises to you.
As no one knows more than you now,
what is as important as breathing and believing.

While doing so, I will ask a question to myself,
somewhere knowing the answers to why
you kept returning to me,

knocking at my heart (when I had my eyes closed),
following me in the mountains
(when I stood there alone, pondering my purpose).

You waited for my return
(when I wasn't sure if I ever would)
from the shred of land we once thrust upon,

and doused with the acid and gels of Napalm.
The very vein of earth now blooms like a lotus
in the dark pond of our consciousness.

When I was picking the bits and pieces of metals
our warriors were made of in the craters left behind by our bombs,
dispensed into the heart of Vietnam, dear Ukraine,

you spoke to me in the language of your soul,
with courage and integrity, approached me graciously,
wrote me the kindest words, invited me

to petition the world to write poems of love,
and put them in the pocket of every warrior headed to
defend your frontiers, whisper them into the ears of demons,

who can't hear the voices of your sufferings. I understand
there is an urgency to write love poems. There is an urgency
to read and listen to poems of love in every corner of the earth.

I can hear your heart beating in anticipation, dear Ukraine,
for the poems I will write for you. The poems
no one has written for anyone ever before.

No one should die without love.
No one should live in its absence.

## Любові вірші до України

Краю милий, я писатиму вірші любові тобі —
ніхто ні для кого таких не писав.

Вразити спроможні вони серед чудес
цього світу. Світу, що допитується до всього,
та нам не дає посутнісних відповідей.

Натомість я виконаю обіцянки тобі.
Адже ніхто не знає більше, ніж ти сьогодні,
що ж є настільки важливим, як дихання і віра.

Водночас себе я спитаю,
знаючи десь уже відповідь:
чому ти весь час повертався до мене,

і стукав у серце мені (я ж заплющила очі),
і переслідував серед гір
(як там залиши́лась сама я, в заду́мі про ціль)?

Ти чекала мого повернення
(коли і не знали, чи повернусь взагалі)
з клаптика землі, на яку ми колись накинулися

і залили отрутами і напалмом.
Справжня вена землі нині розквітає, наче лотос
у темному ставку нашої свідомості.

Коли я відшукувала осколки металу, з якого
наших воїнів створювали, у вирвах від наших бомб,
завислих у серці В'єтнаму, дорога Україно,

від тебе промовили до мене мовою душі,
рішуче і щиро, торкнули мене граційно,
написали теплі слова, попросили

і світ попросити писати любові вірші
і класти їх у кишені воїнів, відправлених
захистити кордони, шепотіти їх у вуха чортам,

які не чують голосів ваших страждань.
Я свідома, що є потреба писати любові вірші.
Є потреба читати і слухати любові вірші по всій землі.

Я чую, як твоє серце б'ється в передчутті, Краю милий,
цих віршів, що тобі їх писатиму. Віршів,
що ніхто ні для кого таких не писав.

Ніхто хай не вмре без любові.
Ніхто хай не живе за її відсутності.

*Авторка ще до російсько-української війни досліджувала феномен війни в американській дійсності та його рецепцію різними верствами населення, осмислюючи В'єтнам, Ірак, Афганістан через безпосереднє спілкування з ветеранами.*

## Your Return

Who would have thought,
I will meet you in time again.
Just in another body,
in a different place, under
similar circumstances.

You were the gift of war,
you are a gift of yet another bloody war,
sent to me wrapped in silk,
painted with red viburnum
from a meadow set on fire.

Your mighty wings want to take me
to another height. I am not scared of heights.
I am just afraid of falling with you from there,
but you aren't. You like diving from the sky
and I close my eyes when you do.

You like doing everything you want for me
without my permission. As if it has
already been granted to you from heaven.
I celebrate your return, my friend.

But yet again, in a hurry!
You have to go. I know.
Here is the cup. Hold it.
You can drink while driving.
It won't break any rules.

But before you enter your home,
don't forget to break my teacup.
Do not forget to shred my poetry
and feed it to the winds.

# Твоє повернення

Подумати хто б тільки зміг,
що я тебе зустріну ще раз.
У тілі іншому,
в місцині незнайомій, хоч
обставини подібні.

Був даром ти війни,
є даром іншої кривавої війни,
мені в шовках надісланим,
розписаних червоною калиною,
з пасовищ у вогні.

Ти крилами могутніми своїми мене бажаєш
на іншу висоту піднéсти. Я не боюсь висот.
Та тільки мені лячно з тобою впасти звідти.
Ні, не впадеш ти. Ти просто плинеш з висі,
і очі я заплющую, коли це робиш.

Тобі робити все, що хочеш, для мене можна
навіть більше, про дозвіл не питай. Оскільки
це вже даровано тобі з небес.
Повернення твоє, мій друже, я святкую.

Та знову поспіх цей!
Тобі потрібно йти, я знаю.
Горнятко — ось. Його візьми.
І можеш пити у дорозі.
Цим не порушиш жодних правил.

Та перед тим, як в дім зайти,
горня розбий.
А вірші, що писала я, порви
і вітрові віддай.

## Fear

Walking with you is like
walking in a field of landmines.
One mistake and everything is finished.
I do not want to lose you over again to another war.

## Страх

З тобою прогулянка —
це хода як по мінному полю.
Помилка єдина — і всьому кінець.
Так не хочу я втратити знову тебе через іншу війну.

## Survival Kit

When nothing else works,
love acts like a balm.
It heals and comforts,
nourishes and assures,
stops insanity,
forbids atrocities.

The mere thought of someone
you hold like a prayer book in your heart,
and read it, despite being
a thousand miles apart,
can spark galaxies—
millions of light years away
when the earth is dark.

You really don't owe me
any explanation for why
you want to read my love poems.
I get it...

Every soldier must carry a survival kit
stashed with love poems written for him.

# Тривожна валіза

Коли вже ніщо не у поміч,
любов є справжнім бальзамом.
Зігріє вона, заспокоїть,
наситить і убезпечить,
зупинить вона божевілля
і стримає від шаленства.

Одна лише думка про того,
хто в серці живе молитвою,
за тисячі миль відчувається,
запалює просто галактики —
із віддалі в мільйони років світлових,
коли ще земля — у темряві.

Тобі не потрібно ніскілечки
мені проясняти причини,
чом вірші любові мої прочитати бажаєш.
Бо знаю чому…

В тривожній валізі солдата є місце
для віршів любові, для нього написаних.

# Defending You

*~ A response to "War. Day One" by Lyudmyla Khersonska*

The war is at your door and
I hear a knock on my window.
I look outside and know what a war looks like.

It looks like a hungry ghost with a big belly,
tiny neck, and narrow throat. It wants to eat
more and more but can't swallow anything.

Thirsty, it pours blood into a chalice
that has no bottom. Its hunger and thirst
can't be satiated.

But I will open my window
to let the beast in, as long as
it promises to leave your door.

I will welcome the Devil in a dress
I bought to wear for you but never did.
I will make him tea to drink with me in silence,

cook him the meals you loved.
I will read him the poems I wrote for you,
but you never read.

I will seduce him with my sweetness,
make him fall in love with me.
I will give him my sword to slay me,

after we make love, so it won't be thirsty
for anyone else's blood.
I will do anything it takes to defend you.

I'll do everything it asks me to do,
but only if it promises to leave your door.
And not to return ever again—dear Ukraine.

## В захисті Тебе

*~ Відповідь на вірш «Війна. День перший» (рос.) Людмили Херсонської*

Війна ось за дверима і
вже чую стукіт у вікно.
Я визираю — знаю вже її подобу.

Вона є привидом із черевом роздутим,
тонкою шиєю й горлянкою вузькою. Вона ізжерти хоче
більше, більше, хоча не може проковтнути все.

Спрагла, вона ллє кров у чашу,
бездонну. І спрагу її й голод
повік не вдовольнити.

Та відчиню я все ж вікно,
щоб звір заліз в мою домівку
за обіцянку закрити за собою двері твоєї.

Зустріну Звіра я у сукні,
для тебе що її придбала (не одягнувши досі).
Зроблю йому гербату (розпити з ним у тиші),

зготую йому страву (що ти любив).
І прочитаю вірші (що їх тобі писала,
тобі і не відомі).

І спокушу його принадами своїми,
примушу пестити мене нестримно.
І дам меча, щоб він забив мене,

наситившись любов'ю, — тим позбавлю його спраги —
шукати свіжу кров.
Зроблю я все, тебе щоб захистити.

Зроблю я все, що він лише попросить,
натомість присягне нехай покинути твій дім
(Назавжди! Без повернення!), о, Україно — Краю милий.

## The Spirit of Ukraine

*~ For President Volodymyr Zelenskyy*

*"When they will come for us, they will see our faces, not the back"*

*"The fight is here; I need ammunition, not a ride"*

When you uttered these words to the maestros of the world
who wanted to prance your war-horses
on their overture, dear Ukraine,
I cheered for you for your courage and defiance.

I felt no remorse for our shattered pride.
Stars and Stripes, let's stop giving rides to friends.
Walk with them. Walk with them in their shoes.
Walk with them barefoot when there is no leather
left on earth to cover our feet.

*The victory belongs to Ukraine.*
*Defeat is not accepted by its braves.*
I contended with my father when Bucha and Mariupol happened.
He hinted the enemy is stronger.
*Surrendering is the best option to avoid more violence.*
And after a pause—*if YOU won't step up to the plate.*

And I roared! *Who am I, father?*
He definitely meant to call me an American,
not Indian, when he addressed me as YOU.

*I wouldn't give a blade of grass from my garden to feed*
*the mouth of this monster. It must crush me under its tank*
*before entering my home. I must jump into a fire pit*
*before it touches my body with its bloody hand.*
But I knew it wasn't my father who was speaking to me.

It was his fear and torment. Our ancestors were returning to him
in his DNA, who were massacred in millions by the murderers;*
who marched like fire ants down the mountains of the Hindukush,
crossing our frontiers, crawling in the sands of *Thar* to enter
our prosperous lands, they were speaking to me through my father.

The wailing of our women and children,
the *Jauhar*** of our queens and princesses,
who jumped into the wells lit with flames
to protect themselves from rape and dishonor,
were returning to him in his speech directed at me.

History lives on and testifies for those who survive.
Our holy chants were extracted from our throats,
our mouths were filled with words to ask for mercy
from our assailants in a language we did not speak.

And those who denied them*** — were made to eat stones,
sit on the iron platter on burning stoves, be thrown in boiling water
in large cauldrons, and buried alive in vaults of stones.
Their memories were returning to my father in his DNA,
passed on to me when he saw me standing with You.

My father didn't really want you to give up, dear Ukraine.
He just wanted your children to survive and thrive through
the perilous journeys of times, as our ancestors did,
and became triumphant.

**Muslim conquests in the Indian subcontinent.*
***The practice of mass self-immolation by women in ancient India to avoid capture, enslavement, and rape by an invading army when facing defeat during a war.*
****The brutality of Mughal rulers against Sikh Gurus, their children, and family.*

# Дух України

*~ Володимиру Зеленському, Президентові України*

*«When they will come for us, they will see our faces, not the back»*

*«The fight is here; I need ammunition, not a ride»*

Як озвучив слова ці
світу цього усім можновладцям,
що воліли твоєї бравади
в їх прелюдіях, дорога Україно,
я вдячна тобі за сміливість і спротив.

Я не мала гризот за підважену гордість.
Зірково-смугасті, припинімо катати партнерів.
Станьмо поруч. У їх черевиках пройдімось.
Босоніж пройдімось, коли між землею і кроком
немає для захисту ніг нічогісінько.

*«Звитяга належить Вкраїні.*
Поразці не місце, коли є відвага».
Я з татусем розсварилася, Маріуполь і Буча як сталися.
Він переконував: «Ворог — сильніший.
Піддатися — вихід найкращий, аби запобігти свавіллю, —
і, помовчавши: — Якщо не вестимешся на провокації».

І я заволала: «Татку, то хто ж я?».
Він чітко означив, що я не індуска —
американка, звернувшись до мене на Ти.

«Я і травинки з подвір'я не дам, аби цього монстра
нагодувати. Йому доведеться танком чавити мене,
аби увійти у будинок. Я швидше стрибну у багаття,
ніж дам цій кривавій руці доторкнутись до тіла».
До мене, це знала я точно, не татко тоді промовляв,

а страх і страждання безсилі. Бо предки уже повернулися
в його ДНК — вбивали мільйонами нас завойовники*,
що з гір Гіндукушу, неначе мурахи, спускалися,
пройшовши кордони, пробравшись через піски, щоб проникнути
в нашу землю родючу — тож через татка вони промовляли до мене.

Плачі всіх наших жінок і дітей,
джаугар** і радживн, і принцес —
у колодязь, себе підпаливши, кидалися,
аби не пізнати ганьби і знеславлення, —
повернулись до нього в його слові до мене.

Історія далі живе й випробовує тих, хто все ж вижив.
Наші гімни святі були вирвані з глоток,
з наших уст виринала тільки мольба про помилування
до завойовників мовою, нам не відомою досі.

А тих, хто мовчав, — годували камінням,
пекли на розпеченій таці з металу, варили в окропі,
ховали живими у склепах камінних***.
Їх спогади в татові, в його ДНК, проявилися зараз,
коли він побачив мене пліч-о-пліч з Тобою.

Насправді татусь не бажав, дорога Україно, твоєї поразки.
А тільки, щоб діти твої залиши́лись живими
у цій доленосній мандрівці, як це наші предки зуміли,
здобувши свою перемогу.

** Головно мусульманське завоювання Індостану відбувалося впродовж XIII–XVIII століть. Проте перший спротив чинили раджпутські князівства ще починаючи з VIII ст. В XI ст. Арабський халіфат підкорив Пенджаб іҐуджарат, а XII ст. сунітська династія Гурідів запанувала в Індії. Впродовж століть різні мусульманські, афганські династії та династії Великих Моголів користалися з роздрібності індуїстських князівств і правили в Делі, аж до часу зміцнення раджпутських династій, усамостійнення навабів Бенгалії і держави сикхів, а також постання князівства майсурів й імперії Маратха у середині XVIII ст. Ці столітні баталії на густонаселеному субконтиненті вважаються найкривавішими у світовій історії.*

*** Джаугар — масове самоспалення жінок в Індії для уникнення полону, рабства чи зґвалтування армією нападника. Вперше задокументоване в часи інвазії Александра Македонського. В часи ісламсько-раджпутських війн вчинялося, коли поразка своїх військ ставала очевидною.*

**** Історія про катування гуру, поета і державного діяча Арджуни Сінга (1563–1606) належить до передань у сикхській традиції. Ймовірним місцем страти є ґурдвара (місце служіння сикхів, своєрідний храм) у Лахорі, сучасний Пакистан. Впродовж п'яти днів звинуваченого в проповідуванні «нетакого послання до Бога» позбавляли їжі, питва та сну (день 1-й), варили в казані (день 2-й), обпікали розпеченим піском (день 3-й), смажили на пательні (день 4-й), зашивали у волячу шкіру (день 5-й). У всіх випробовуваннях гуру сидів спокійно, не відчуваючи болю, і лише зосереджувався на Вахіґуру, на вищій божественній силі, про якого йому звістив Нанак, а також на ґурбані, сикхських гімнах, у яких присутній звук безпосередньо від Всевишнього. Він виносив тортури, щоб подати приклад, як не втрачати терпіння і не зневажати Бога у стражданнях, у найсправжнішому випробуванню віри.*

## Ground Zero

Splitting the lungs of the sky
a shell drops like an hourglass of fire,
on the heart of Zaporizhzhia,
emptying itself to the last atom.

The hole left in the heart of the earth
fills with the cries of millions
fleeing their homes...
Every heart in a war is ground zero.

## Рівень нуля

Розколюючи легені неба,
всяка бомба падає піском у годиннику
вогненнім на серце Запоріжжя,
спустошуючись до останнього атома*.

Вирву, залишену в серці землі,
заповнюють крики мільйонів,
які покидають оселі…
На війні кожне серце — на рівні нуля.

** 4 березня 2022 року російські окупаційні сили атакували український Енергодар, місце розташування найбільшої в Європі Запорізької АЕС. Запис із камер спостереження системи безпеки ЗАЕС облетів увесь світ — провідні ЗМІ подали фотокадри вибухів поблизу реакторів. Цей ядерний тероризм-шантаж Москви мав за мету посіяти паніку, насамперед в Європі, та стимулювати світ примусити Київ припинити спротив, капітулювати та стати маріонетковим псевдодержавним утворенням під повним контролем Кремля. ЗАЕС контролюється московськими спецслужбами та «Росатомом» уже рік, енергоблоки переведені в заморожений режим функціонування. МАГАТЕ з літа 2022 року робить поки що безуспішні спроби з демілітаризації зони навколо ЗАЕС, тим самим Москва зберігає за собою можливість ядерного шантажу на мирному об'єкті.*

## Sunflower

I draw a sunflower in the sand and toss it up into the sky.

Grab it if you can, and hand it to that little Ukrainian boy
walking alone, in tears, toward the border of a foreign land.

The plastic bag he carries, has a message for the world.
The red diary he holds has the offenses of history.

The burdens on his shoulders are ours.
He is tired—give him the flower.

He stops suddenly, refusing to walk
in the direction, the world is going.

In his *halt* are the hopes for the future.

## Сонях

Малюю сонях я на піску, затим підкидаю його увись —

зловіть, якщо зможете, і передайте хлопчикові з України,
що йде сам-один, у сльозах, до кордону з чужою землею.

В пластмасовім ранці несе він до світу послання.
В щоденнику багрім — жахіття історії.

Тягар на плечах його — наш, поза сумнівом.
Він перевтомився —тож дайте ту квітку йому.

Ураз зупиняється, йти відмовляючись далі,
він у керунку, якого тримається світ.

В його завмиранні — надії на будучність.

## War: A One Way Street

Driving in my town,
I imagine sirens blaring, tanks rolling,
and guns pointing at people resisting.

I see no dove flying in the sky.
The olive trees are eradicated from
every corner of the earth.

I shiver in fear, like a leaf on an amputated branch.
My children are home, but I can't turn around.
War is a one-way street. We can only pull back.

The hospitals are filled with injured and burnt bodies.
The buildings and homes are engulfed in fire.
I have no weapon to fight. I may not return home tonight.

War is a phenomenon, the accumulation of our thoughts and actions.
What goes on in our minds, manifests in the world.

The idea of who we are is not limited to our narrow discretion.
I'm a person, and a nation, an ally, and an adversary.

I'm a woman raped and mutilated by my enemies,
and a limb hanging from the window of a building struck.

I'm a fallen soldier who died defending his country.
And my slayer does not know what he is fighting for.

I am bent like the little girl, pulled up by force on the last train
about to leave the station, bound to a foreign land.

I'm the agony of a father in exodus, without his sons and daughters.
I'm a sorrow, frozen in the eyes of a young girl who presses her palm

against the windowpane of a train, to touch the hands of the men
staying behind to fight for their country.

I'm the blood-crusted snow after a night of
heavy shelling, on my falling city.

There is no glory in a war. Every home has a shrine.
A war cannot be defined. It can only be lived or imagined.

## Війна: в один бік

За кермом у своєму місті я уявляю
завивання сирен, гуркіт танків, а також
всю зброю, націлену на оборонців.

Жодного голуба в небі не бачу я.
Оливні дерева зрубані під корінь
по всіх кінцях світу.

Тремчу я в страху, мов листок на зрізаній гілці.
Діти удома, та не можу до них повернутись.
Рух на війні — односторонній: нам доводиться тільки відходити.

Медустанови заповнені раненими і обпаленими.
Будинки й хати спалені всі дотла.
Не маю зброї, щоб битися. І, може, не повернуся нині додому.

Війна є феноменом, концентрацією думок і дій наших.
Те, що у головах наших, стає дійсністю в світі.

З'ясування «Хто ми?» не обмежується сховком нашим вузьким.
Я — людина, я — народ, я — альянт і я — супротивник.

Я — жінка, зґвалтована і змордована ворогами,
і кінцівка звисає з вікна будинку, снарядом розтрощеного.

Я — полеглий солдат, що впав, захищаючи землю.
А мій вбивця навіть не знає, за що він воює.

Я скоцюрблена, наче дівчатко, запхане в останній потяг
перед відправленням, що прямує до чужої землі.

Я — немочі батька в цій масовій втечі, що залишив тут донь і синів.
Я — смуток, застиглий в оченятах дівчатка, яка притискає долоньку

до скла, аби поєднати її із рукою мужчини,
який боронити країну лишається.

Я — зашерхлий в крові сніг після ночі
масивного обстрілу мого міста, що гине.

Жодної величі у війні. В кожній оселі — вже пам'яті сховок.
Війну годі визначити — тільки прожити або уявити.

## The One With Her Lion

Here she comes down from the mountains onto your plains.
Her lion roars in the face of your enemies on your battlefields,
following her move and every step.

She holds a trident in one hand and a heap of lotus
and sunflowers in her other.
The dawn is breaking from the center of her brow.

Her hair is washed with the water of your twenty-three thousand rivers
and fragrant with the scent of your winds, dear Ukraine.
She vows not to tie her long, dark hair flowing from

the mountain of Hoverla to the Sea of Azov
until the last ship of your enemy is driven off from your waters
and every teardrop is wiped from the faces of your children.

Today she will clear the battlefields with you,
lay a sunflower on the coffin of every soldier
who sacrificed their life to protect your honor.

Clad in yellow and blue, she has arrived at your invitation.
The letters you wrote her like prayers have now become
the Mantras reverberating through the land of Skovoroda.

You aren't alone. She is here to adorn you with
all the weapons you need
to protect your land, dear Ukraine.

She is here with her sword, axe, and club, multiplied into millions,
a bowl full of food, enough to feed the entire universe till eternity.
Your children will never go hungry.

She is going nowhere until the victory is yours.
She will be here to fight the last battle against the demons,
from this to the other end of the universe.

And the day the triumph will be yours,
she will blow her conch shell to declare your victory
from the highest peak of your land.

She is none other than you, dear Ukraine!
In her heart swelled with pride for you,
she carries your songs, humming them

like the sounds of the cosmos
filling time and space as you rest.
Your peaceful breaths — falling into her warm embrace.

*"The One With Her Lion" refers to Mother Goddess Durga, also known as the War Goddess and the slayer of demons.*

## Та сама, зі своїм левом*

Вона спустилася із гір в твої степи.
І лев ричить на ворогів із бойовищ твоїх
за кожним її рухом, кожним кроком.

Вона тримає тризуб у руці, а в іншій —
квітку лотоса і сонях.
Світанок між бровами згаснув враз.

Її волосся тисячі твоїх річок — їх двадцять три — водою омиває,
а пахощі приносять твої вітри, о люба Україно.
Вона вже присягла своє волосся (чорне, довге, аж від Говерли

і до Азову) не зв'язувати аж до часу, доки
на дно останній піде корабель ворожий
й кожнісінька сльоза твоїх дітей отримає одвіт.

Вона з тобою нині вже очистить бойовища
і сонях покладе на домовину кожного солдата,
який офірував своє життя, щоб захистити честь твою.

Вона, обвита в жовто-синє, вже тут на поклик твій.
Листи — твої моли́тви— нині стали мантрами
й відлунюють по всій землі Сковороди.

Ти — не сама. Вона є тут, аби прикрасити
тебе всією зброєю, якої потребуєш ти
для захисту земель твоїх, о Краю милий.

Тут є вона з мечем, сокирою і булавою, все до мільйонів
збільшила, з поживою у чаші — вистачить нагодувати світ повік.
Ніколи твої діти не пізна́ють вже часів голодних.

Вона не зникне, поки ти не переможеш.
В останній битві проти зла вона з тобою поруч,
наприкінці як цього світу, так і іншого, коли той буде.

І день тріумфу за тобою назавжди́ залишить,
і засурмить вона у горн морський, аби звістити про твою
звитягу із найвищої вершини твоїх земель.

Вона насправді — це є ти, о Краю милий!
За тебе гордістю вже сповнена її душа,
вона несе твої пісні і їх наспівує

у звуках космосу,
заповнивши собою і час, і простір в мить, коли відпочиваєш.
Ти мирно дихаєш в теплі її обіймів.

** Дурга («недосяжна», «непереможна») — одна з форм Деві, індуїстської богині, праматір усіх богинь і винищувачка демонів, зображувалася десятирукою, усміхненою, верхи на леві, озброєною, з квіткою лотоса, під час виконання мудр (ритуальних жестів).*

## Call Me Uyava

Your love, sheer light,
cuts the darkness like a diamond*
that can never be stolen by
the occupiers of your land.

But who am I to be worthy of your diamond?
I do not know the answer to it.
I am born only with questions
and have found no answer to any of them.

I have been drifting in celestial storms
for eternity, seeking answers to my questions.
I am a seeker, searching for myself.
I have no name or identity of my own.

Everything that I have, is borrowed from the universe.
I own nothing. I have borrowed from you too.
But when I can't remember. It has been long. So long.
Now I'm here, to hand you over everything, with love,

that you once gifted me in abundance. Only because
I can't possibly carry them in my tiny bowl of alms.
Allow me to cover your wounds, as they are my own.
Let me stay to celebrate your victory. As it will be mine too.

I have followed your light to come home.
But I do not know where I come from,
what's my name. Dear Ukraine,
you can call me—*Uyava!*

**Diamond that cuts through illusion. "Diamond Sutra" is a sermon given by the Buddha.*
*https://plumvillage.org/library/sutras/the-diamond-that-cuts-through-illusion/*

*Uyava (уява) means "imagination" in the Ukrainian language.*

## Називай мене Уявою

Любов твоя сяє велично.
Вона розрізає цю темінь, немов діамантова сутра*,
яку не по силі нікому загарбати,
нехай там який окупант.

А хто я така, аби із твоїм діамантом зрівнятися?
Не знаю одвіту на це.
Від народин у мене питання постійні,
і жодних одвітів на них не знайшла.

Я дрейфую в небесному штормі,
віками уже, на питання одвіти аби віднайти.
У пошуку я, і себе в першу чергу.
Назватися як, я не знаю.

Від всесвіту все, що моє, я у позику взя́ла.
Я не маю за власне нічого. Позичала я в тебе також.
Та коли, не згадаю. Тривало це довго. Задовго.
І тепер я є тут, щоб віддати тобі із любов'ю

геть усе, чого набула я від тебе сповна. Лиш тому,
що не можу нести це усе у чаші малій із офірою.
Загоїти рани твої, наче власні мої, я бажаю, дозволь.
Бути поруч дай змогу у час, як прийде́ перемога. Бо вона і моя.

Я за світлом твоїм шлях додому знайшла.
Та не знаю, звідкіль ця дорога була
і яким є у мене ім'я. Краю милий,
мене називай ти Уявою!

* *Діамантова сутра, «Сутра про досконалу мудрість, що розрізає [ілюзію, темряву невігластва], як удар блискавки», — основоположний текст буддизму, створений бл. III ст. н. е.*

## Misspelling

I

"We are sick of telling the world,
how to spell our names correctly!"
"Vladimir is Russian, and Volodymyr is Ukrainian,
Do you get it?"

Yes, and I am sorry!
I know why you feel so deeply hurt.
I own my mistake and am willing to correct it.
I didn't realize that someday in our world,
misspelling a name would cause so much hurt.

Both brothers are mine.
One is an angel, another a devil,
made by the same God, fed by the same earth.
The same blood runs through their veins.
The meanings of their names—exactly the same!

Yet, I ask for your forgiveness.
Please, forgive me, dear Ukraine!

# Перекрут

## I

«Ми втомились волати на цілий цей світ —
Імена називайте коректно —
У Росії — Владімір, Володимир — у нас,
Хіба зрозуміти це складно?»

Так, я бачу й поправлю цю річ відсьогодні.
Знаю я вже, щó саме тобі так болить.
Визнаю я помилку, її я усуну.
Хто б раніше подумав, що імен плутанина
є причиною болю такого в житті?

Брат і брат є моїми.
Перший — ангел, а інший — дияволом став.
Та обоє сотворені Богом єдиним, і обох їх зростила єдина земля.
Кров у жилах тече одна й та сама.
І однакове значення їхніх імен.

Так, я про прощення прошу тебе:
 будь ласкавий, прости, Краю милий!

# Misspelling

## II

I may not know how to spell your name.
But I know what it means.
It means a lot to me.

# Перекрут

## II

Я можу і не знати, як вимовити твоє ім'я.
Та я знаю, щó воно означає.
Означає для мене воно так багато.

## Promise

Every soldier has a poet
hidden in his heart, often killed in friendly fire.

Those who return home to write—
their verses must be fed to the children
with their mother's breast milk.

They must be taught to the students in classrooms.
They must be preached at places of worship.
They must be read to the entire humankind

from the highest point on earth.
No one can write the verses a soldier can,
to keep the sanctity of humanity.

Promise me, my warrior, my friend,
you will bring me back your poet when you return.

## Обіцянку

Кожен воїн — поетом у власному серці,
незнаним, ураженим дружнім вогнем.

Віршам тих, хто повертається додому писати,
належить поживою стати для немовлят
нарівні із грудним молоком матерів.

Ними належить навчати студентів на парах.
Ними належить молитви підносити в храмах.
Ними належить звертатись до людства усього

з найвищої точки планети.
Оскільки ніхто не напише так віршів, як зможе солдат,
щоб людяність людство змогло зберегти.

Обіцянку дай мені, друже мій, воїне,
ти, повернувшись, поета мені принесеш.

## Ancient Wound

When I'm supposed to write
loads and loads of love poems
to deliver to your frontiers, dear Ukraine,

I am writing a speech like a politician,
a lecture like a professor.
I'm sharing my vision like a philosopher.

But all I want at the moment, is to fly away,
like a heron in a peaceful sky, leaving no traces behind,
carrying a bullet in my chest like you—ancient, divine.

## Давня рана

Як маю потребу писати
стоси і стоси віршів любові,
аби до границь твоїх їх, Краю милий, дїслати,

промову пишу я подібно політикові,
чи подібно професору лекцію.
Свій погляд я ширю подібно філософу.

Та все, що я хочу в цю мить, — відлетіти,
мов чапля до мирного неба, без сліду позаду,
із кулею в грудях подібно тобі — священною, давньою.

## Would You?

*~ Inspired by Buddha's life story, Siddhartha and the Swan*

A swan shot with an arrow
breathes faintly in the hands of a warrior
and asks him, would you be my *Siddhartha*?*

Would you rescue me or send me back to
the one who has shot this arrow into my chest,
and left me bleeding?

I couldn't evade my destiny, as a swan gifted with
a tranquil heart and the beauty of snowy wings,
now drenched in my blood.

How can beauty instigate such cruelty?
You must find an answer to it
when you are enlightened someday,

under my *Bodhi Tree.***

**Siddhartha, a Kshatriya prince from Shakya clan, who became the Buddha.*
***Bodhi Tree, under which the Buddha got enlightened, is located in Bodhgaya, Bihar, India.*

## Чи зробиш?

*~ на оповідь про Сіддгартху і Лебідку*

Лебідка зі стрілою в тілі
на воїна руках ледь дихає,
його питаючи: «Сіддгартхою для мене будеш?

Спасеш? Чи віддаси тому,
чия стріла у мене в грудях,
аби спливала кров'ю я?

Своєї долі не уникну, як та лебідка, обдарована
серденьком смирним і красою сяйних крил,
тепер скривавлених без міри.

Чому жорстокість аж таку спричинює краса?
Тобі одвіт знайти прийде́ться,
як світлом сповнишся колись,

під деревом Бодгі моїм».

*1. Сіддгартха, раджпутський принц із клану кшатріїв, пізніше — Будда.*
*2. Білу лебідку підстрілив брат Сіддгартхи, але поранена птаха потрапила до рук Сіддгартхи. Брат, звісно, став вимагати, аби впольоване віддали йому.*

# Phoenix

We sound like empty drums
in the stillness of night
on the continents divided.

Hold my hands, my friend,
look into my eyes until
the sun rises on my forehead
to burn me in its flames.

Let all the birds of my dreams
fly away from the nests of my eyes.
There is no way for such a love to survive.

If there is another day, another life,
I promise to rise like a Phoenix
from the ashes of my being
in your skies, blue and yellow.

## Фенікс

Лунаємо в тиші нічній,
розділеній на континенти,
так гучно, немов барабани.

Візьми мої руки, мій друже,
заглянь в мої очі, аби на чолі
побачити сонце як сходить,
мене щоб спалити до тла.

Дозволь всім птахам моїх мрій
відлетіти із гнізд — із очей.
Немає інших шляхів для любові, щоб вижити.

Якщо є інший день, якщо є життя інше,
як Фенікс я обіцяю постати
із попелу свого буття
у небі твоїм, синьо-жовтім.

## Your Words

I hear the words you say and free them
with a blown kiss like the seeds of
a dandelion flower in the wind.

It isn't that they do not matter.
They mean everything.

But everything is nothing in the end.
The core of an atom is empty
like my longing heart.

## Твої слова

Я чую слова, ти кажеш які, і їх вивільняю
тендітним цілунком подібно до цвіту
кульбабки на вітрі.

І не через те, що байдужа до них я.
Вони для мене — все.

Та усе є нічим врешті-решт.
Ядро атома спорожніле
подібно до мого спраглого серця.

## Psalms

I hear the words you do not say,
write them in my notebook
and listen to them, like Psalms.

## Псалми

«Я чую слова, яких ти не кажеш,
пишу їх у записнику
і слухаю, наче Псалми».

## The Alchemist

Trust me, I did try to ruin everything,
over again. I even tried calling the alchemist
who always invents a new formula
to put my joy to sleep and cause my body
untouched by time, to go limp.

But he wasn't a help either.
He hung up, after asking me, "*Who is this?*"
I know it has been twelve years...
A lot of things can be forgotten in that time,
but not the address to your home,
not the faces you kiss
and write death sentences for them.

But obviously, this is what happened.
It's a totally different time for me.
It's possible he wasn't able to see
my face in the light where I stood,
as we always met in dark meadows.

But when you ask a question to someone,
please wait at least to hear the answer
before hanging up.

Maybe, someone has a more urgent need than dying.
Maybe, this time, someone just wanted to live.

## Алхімік

Повір мені, я прагнула все зруйнувати,
знову. Алхіміку дзвонила навіть,
бо формулу нову знаходив зáвжди він,
аби приспати мою радість і зробити тіло,
якого не торкнувся час, оспалим.

…Не допоміг. І від’єднався,
спитавши тільки: «Дзвонить хто?».
Дванадцять літ злетіло, знаю
За час забути можна все,
окрім адреси твого дому,
окрім облич, які цілуєш
і пишеш їм смертні вироки.

Та, видно, сталось саме так.
Для мене це інакший вимір.
Ймовірно, він моє обличчя
не зміг при світлі розпізнати,
бо перед цим на темних луках ми зустрічались.

Але коли ви ставите комусь питання,
будь ласка, зачекайте хоча б на відповідь,
перш ніж покласти слухавку.

Можливо, хтось має більш нагальну потребу, ніж смерть.
Можливо, цього разу хтось просто хотів жити.

# Ring of Fire

No one could dare enter the ring of fire
I created it with my penance. No bird, no rattle,
no animal, no human could ever break into
the circle of flames that I kept ablaze.
But you did. Who are you?

Why are you here? What do you want from me?
You aren't God, you aren't an angel either.
Then who are you? Whirling under the roof of the sky
on a starry night, she asked this question to him
over and over again.

Tell me, O Warrior!
Have you lost your way? Are you hungry or thirsty?
Do you need my help with finding your lost horses?
What do you need? Tell me, how did you end up
in this dense forest to be with me, alone?

This wasn't supposed to happen.
I was supposed to live and die alone.
Loveless and painless having no one around me.
But you cracked the code and entered my soul without a sound.
Without burning yourself, without turning into ashes.

But he remained silent,
put his sword down and knelt before her
with his gaze low. But I am not your queen!
She cautioned him. Tell me, O Warrior,
how did you enter my chamber built with walls of fire?

Why is this humility before me?
Are you here to save me or slay me with love?
She asked these questions to him all night
orbiting like the earth until he rose like the sun
on her mountains, turning her into a river.

# Круг вогню

Ніщо з живого навіть близько не змогло ввійти у круг
вогню, що я створила як покуту. Ні птах, ані гримучник,
ні звір, ані людина не спромоглися розірвати
той круг вогню, що запалила я.
Спромігся ти. Тож хто ти?

Чому ти тут? Чого від мене хочеш?
Ти не Господь, не ангел навіть.
Отож хто ти? В крутінні під склепінням неба,
зірками всіяного, все вона питала
його, повторюючись.

О воїне, скажи мені!
Ти збився зі стезі? Бажаєш їсти, пити?
Потрібна допомога, аби знайти твоїх загублених коне́й?
Що хочеш врешті-решт? Скажи мені, як сталося, що ти
в густому лісі опинився сам-на-сам зі мною?

Ніщо цього не провіщало.
Мені судилося життя і смерть в самотності.
Ні почуттів, ні болю, адже нікого поруч.
Та ти зламав замок і увійшов у глибину душі без звуку.
Не обпалившись, попелом не ставши.

Однак мовчав він.
Поклав свій меч і вклякнув перед нею
з очима вділ. Тобі не королева я!
Йому вона звістила. Скажи, о воїне,
ввійшов ти як в мої палати, якщо з вогню я стіни будувала?

Чому оцю смиренність бачу зараз?
Ти тут, аби мене спасти чи вразити на смерть любов'ю?
Вона всю ніч його про це питала
в невпиннім русі, мов земля, аж поки він, подібно сонцю
на її вершинах, її перетворив на річку.

# The Spirit of a Warrior

You don't go looking for love. It finds you.
Even when its eyes are closed, it recognizes you.

It makes its way to you like a firefly,
not afraid of your flame or the circle of fire
you have created to protect yourself.

It breaks every ring of fire to touch your flame.
It's an act of bravery and the one who takes upon
this challenge has the spirit of a warrior.

No matter how long it takes, it finds you.
No matter how far you stay, it covers all distance
to kiss your flame and die for you at once.

You can't resist. You can't evade.
It follows the scent released in the air
when you burn like a candle waiting for love.

It comes transcending all barriers, crossing all borders
to siphon the poison you have been inhaling.
It is oxygen for your lungs, collapsing.

It is the most essential item to carry in your pack
when you are headed to war.

## Правдивий дух воїна

Любові не шукаєш ти — вона тебе знайшла.
Заплющені у неї очі — хай — тебе вона впізнала.

Вона свій шлях до тебе прокладає, мов світлячок,
що не боїться полум'я твого чи кола із вогню,
який накреслив ти, щоб захиститись.

Вона здолає кожне коло вогню, аби торкнутись
твого горіння. Це мужній чин, і кожен, хто цей виклик
приймає, має воїна правдивий дух.

На час який — байдуже, головне — тебе знайдé.
На віддалі якій — байдуже, бо вона всі віддалі здолає
заради поцілунку твого вогню і спалення тебе заради.

Не зможеш встояти. Не зможеш утекти.
Вона ледь чутний аромат уловить у повітрі,
коли горітимеш ти наче свічка, що чекає на любов.

Вона приходить, подолавши всі бар'єри, перетнувши
всі межі, щоб отруту вивести, яку вдихав ти.
Вона є киснем для твоїх легенів, що розпадаються.

Вона — найважливіша річ в твоїм обмундируванні,
в якому ти рушаєш на війну.

## Three and a Half Hours

For three and a half hours,
she wrote songs on sand and water.

For three and a half hours, the Pacific winds
carried them to his black sea.

For three and a half hours, fire fell from his skies,
and she fetched her rain clouds to his nation in flames.

For three and a half hours, they prayed, not knowing
if God and angels were listening.

For three and a half hours, their hearts tolled
like the bells in their cathedral and monastery.

For three and a half hours, they watered the seeds of
their dreams and compassion for each other in their eyes.

Someday, they will grow to bear flowers, fruits,
and shade in their lands, wounded and blessed.

For three and a half hours, they looked at each other and smiled,
without blinking their eyes. As if the one who blinks first will lose.

For three and a half hours, he asked her questions of lifetimes
and made his confessions to her.

For three and a half hours, she answered all his questions
and dismissed his misdemeanors.

For three and a half hours, they sat in a dreamlike state
as solid as a mountain, with rivers flowing in their cups.

In three and a half hours, they cruised through the mazes of
centuries and lifetimes, crossing the gates of the heavens.

*Check, check, check.* When every single box in
their hearts had been checked, the access to paradise

was granted them by the universe
to live the moments rare on earth.

## Три і пів години

Три і ще пів години
писала вона пісні на піску і воді.

Три і ще пів години вітри з Тихого
доносили їх до його Чорного моря.

Три і ще пів години з його неба вогонь
спадав, а вона хмари з дощем несла для його народу.

Три і ще пів години молились вони, і не знаючи,
чи Бог і ангели слухають.

Три і ще пів години серця їхні билися так,
наче дзвони у їхніх соборах і лаврах.

Три і ще пів години насіння бажань і симпатії,
що линули з поглядів їхніх, вони поливали.

Час прийде — і виростуть квіти, плоди
і тінь на полях їх країв, поранених, благословенних.

Три і ще пів години без сторонніх очей
вони посміхались і, начебто, грались, хто першим моргне.

Три і ще пів години питав про життя
він її і робив їй на натомість зізнання.

Три і ще пів години на всі запитання
вона відповіла і провини прощала.

Три і ще пів години купались у мріях,
тверді, мов гора, а ріки текли в їхніх чашах.

Три і ще пів години лабіринти віків і життя
долали вони крізь небесні ворота.

Звіт, звіт, звіт. Як перевірили закутки всі
у серцях, доступ до раю їм всесвіт

подарував, аби на землі
прожити оці неповторні миттєвості.

## The One Who Loves

Since when has the sun begun to rise
in the night sky of California?
Good morning, dear soldier!
Do you see the moon rising
in the morning sky of Kharkiv?

What is magical about this unprecedented time is
the gift of love. Writing love letters to Ukraine
at 4:30 in the morning is like being sixteen
and falling asleep on the shoulder of a soldier
a new ZSU recruit, only seventeen,
traveling alone in a tram,
whom I met on Facebook the other day,
who proudly holds his rifle close to his chest
in a picture to die for. *Where had you been
all these years?* I ask. But shy,
he wouldn't respond.

No romantic dates for us,
no meeting in the parks,
but right there, where
he gets into a street fight
in the alleys of Ukraine,
with someone
speaking Russian,
where missiles rained,
sparing just two of us.

Now we meet in no man's land, and he
tries to decipher the language of my heart
by meditating on the words written on
the palms of my hands with henna
in my language, he doesn't know.

But in my dream interrupted—
I wake up six thousand miles away from him
with the sounds of air raid sirens
dropped by him on my phone,
on the yellow coast of the Pacific,
drenched in blue, the colors of his flag
that he proudly wears on his coat of arms.

I mean, who thinks of someone when
the fire is about to rain from the sky?
The one who loves, the one who cares,
the one who has overcome his fears,
the one who has lost sense of his safety
and lives in madness to think
that love can rescue anything,

that love can be his armor
and the weapon to avenge,
that love can be a gospel
to save many a lost soul,
and those, who weren't loved
and died for their nation.

## Той, хто любить

Відколи сонце сходить
посеред ночі у Каліфорнії?
Добрий ранок, дорогий мій солдате!
Ти бачиш у ранковім небі Харкова,
як сходить місяць?

Чарує що в цей час, незнаний досі, —
так це любові дар. Писати Україні ці листи любові
о пів на п'яту ранку — це у шістнадцять наче
заснути на плечі солдата незнайомого —
до війська щойно взятого в сімнадцять —
в поїздці у трамваї,
якого я зустріла у фейсбуці якось —
на грудях автомат тримає гордо на знимці —
за такого вмерти можна. «Де всі роки
ти був раніше?» — його питаю.
Та марно — сором'язливий він — не відповість.

Ані романтики побачень,
ані прогулянок у парках
у нас — а тільки бійка
на вулиці зі стрічним з України,
який промовив
російською
одне—два слова в час,
коли дощить ракетами,
нас, тільки двох нас, оминаючи.

Та нині на нічийних землях ми зустрічаємось,
і прагне він розшифрувати серця мову
мого, міркуючи про слово,
що на долонях рук моїх я написала
хною на мові, що її не знає він.

Та урвались мрії —
за шість тисяч миль від нього збудилась я —
виття сирени про тривогу
у слухавці моїй прорвалось
на жовтий берег океану, залитий синню, —
у барви прапора, що на шевроні
він носить з гордістю.

Собі я твердю: хто думає про когось,
коли вогонь ось-ось впаде із неба?
Той тільки, любить хто, і дбає хто,
хто подолав страхи свої,
хто втратив відчуття безпеки
і втратив голову, міркуючи:
спроможна врятувати все любов,

йому любов — броня,
його відплати зброя,
любов — євангельська новина,
для душ загублених спасіння
і тих, кого і не любили
і хто загинув за народ.

## Gracias, Mi Amigo!

You weave sweaters for my poems
with your words, with the yarns of
your language, with the beads of
your tangled breaths,
seeking freedom.

The freedom of your country
the freedom of your soul,
the freedom of your desires,
on harsh Winter nights,
against the forces—brute and cold.

I know this is one way to survive,
but living is far more important.
I know you care, my friend.
Don't you lie!
I just want to let you know—

when you do this, the universe is warm.

## Gracias, Mi Amigo!

Ти светри плетеш для моїх віршів
зі слів своїх, із пряжі мови власної,
із намистин, із дихання
завивин,
у пошуках свободи.

Свободи для країни,
свободи для душі,
свободи для жадань,
у цій ночі зимовій, лютій,
у відсічі потузі злій, нещадній.

Я знаю, вижити аби, це шлях,
однак самé життя вагоміше, це ж ясно,
я знаю, ти піклуєшся, мій друже.
Не зрадь собі!
Я тільки хочу, аби ти знав —

від дій твоїх тепліє в цілім світі.

## The Last Will be First

And one day, she wore
blue flowers in her hair and
he traveled to the valleys of
her lost dreams, in the Himalayas,
its peaks, covered with snow and
rivers sparkling like their hearts
to fetch blooms, rare and fragrant,
dipped in yellow-gold to adorn her.

Put them together, would you?
And she wore flowers of both colors
in her dark hair to brighten his dark days.

He sent her a blown kiss,
in admiration, and unfurled her
into the heights of the sky,
like his victory flag.
Even in love, he never loved
anyone more than you, dear Ukraine,
and your pride—yellow and blue,

And she was joyous to be the last,
when he said to her—someday,
*first will be last, and the last will be first.* *

**Matthew 19:29-30.*

## Останні будуть першими

І одного дня вплела вона
сині квіти у волосся, а
він помандрував у долини
її втрачених мрій, у Гімалаї,
на їх вершини, що вкриті снігами і
ріками, що іскряться так, як і їхні серця,
щоб рідкісний і ароматний принести
цвіт в позолоті*, аби її вбрати.

Збери їх, зможеш?
І барв обох квіти носила вона
у темнім волоссі, щоб скрасити йому темні дні.

Він повітряний поцілунок їй надіслав
у захопленні, розгорнувши її
у висі небесній,
неначе свій стяг перемоги.
І закоханим він нікого не любив
більше, аніж тебе, дорога Україно,
і гордість твою — жовто-синю.

І запишалась вона, що буде останньою,
коли сказав їй: колись
і *з перших останніми стануть, а останні першими***.

* *Жовто-золотий колір квітки.*

** *Єв. від Матвія 19:30.*

## Saffron Love

*~ Inspired by the Rajasthani folk song "Kesariya Balam" (Saffron Love) written for Rajput warriors for their return home from war*

O my saffron love, in ornate silver
and stripes gold and blue!
I have no clue how our paths crossed,
when every track on earth is torn
and bridges between nations are burnt.

All I know is that we met without meeting.
Stood together in separation, with no earth
beneath our feet. We only have the immensity of
the sky under which I lie like a luminous pearl,
fallen from the shell of your heart.

I no longer look at the lines on the palms
of my hand that wrote my destiny.
I am soaked in silver of moonlight.
I am gold in the glow of the sun. I'm blue,
like the heart of the Pacific when you aren't here.

I am drenched in your colors and have become
the talk of the town. I hear people say—
I am bewildered by your love. I wander into your
mountains and steppes, looking for you. I search for you
barefoot in the blazing desert of *Thar,* my brave land.

Like a princess of an era gone by, I write songs,
like long shadows cast on the dunes by evening sun,
and ask the winds to deliver my messages to you
on your battlefields. And I don't know for sure—
whether I am dead or alive in our days of separation.

I split into pieces on the rocks of my *Aravalli*
and ask my heart to stop beating if you can't hear it.
I collect the embers of the *sol* rising on the horizon
and burn little by little all day. I wreck the ashes of
the setting sun, and the sand swallows all I find.

What other choices do I have than hitting my head
against the rocks and perishing? Tell me, how long is

the sentence of separation, my friend? I promise myself
not to speak to you a thousand times, but what else to try
when my heart no longer listens to me and defies?

We cannot unite, but we can't be separated either.
And I do not know if we have a future. The world talks about
our love, but does not see the pangs of separation—
the only affliction of my heart that can't be cured.
I stand alone on the edge of my desolate land,

waiting for you, with my desert songs,
O my saffron love, in ornate silver
and stripes gold and blue!
I have no clue how we crossed paths,
how we met and fell in love.

*Rajputs: A warrior class during times of war and rulers during peace, in India.*

## Шафранова любов

*~ на раджастанську народну пісню «Kesariya Balat» (шафранове кохання), яку для раджпутських воїнів створили їхні дружини та кохані з нагоди їх повернення з війни*

О моя шафранова любове, убрана в срібло
і в стрічки синьо-золоті!
Не маю я і гадки, сталось як, що наші ці стежки
переплелися в той час, як на землі усі дороги
розривають і спалюють мости поміж народами.

Я знаю тільки: ми зустрілись і не зустрівшись.
Землі немає під ногами, хоч стоїмо разом не поруч.
Над нами лиш одне безмежжя
небес, а під ними я перлиною сіяю,
упавши з мушлі твого серця.

На лінії, що долею порізали мої долоні,
я більше не дивлюся.
Сіяння срібне місячне мене пронизує.
Проміння сонячне мене золотить. Я у блакиті,
мов серце океану Тихого, коли тебе немає тут.

Я пройнялася барвами твоїми, про що
йде поголос у всьому місті. Я чую, щó говорять люди, —
любов'ю спантеличена твоєю. Шукаючи тебе, обходжу я
усі твої степи і гори. Вдивляюся в піски блискучі Тару —
аби знайти твій босий слід, моя звитяжна земле.

Подібно до принцеси із доби минулої пісні співаю я,
що стеляться на дюнах у призахідному сонці, наче тіні,
вітрів питаю я, чи донесли мої листи тобі
на бойовища. І я не знаю точно,
чи мертва я, а чи живу в ці дні розлуки.

Я розриваюсь на шматки на скелях Аравaллі*
і прóшу серце зупинитись, якщо його не чуєш ти.
Збираю я солярні крихти жару над горизонтом
і спалюю поволі їх у плині дня. Розвіюю я попіл по
заходу сонця, і пісок поглинає все, що я знаходжу.

Що залишається мені, окрім як головою об камінь
битись, згинувши опісля? Скажи мені, мій друже, скільки

тягтиметься розлука? Обіцяю собі я неперервно: більше
не говорити жодних слів до тобе, Але що ще можна спробувати,
коли моє серце вже не слухає мене і непокоряється?

З'єднатися — не можемо, та порізно не можемо
ми бути, тож не знаю я, чи є у нас майбутнє. Світ говорить,
яка любов у нас, не бачачи страждань, що ми — окремо,
і серця мого біль нічим вже не зцілити.
Залишена одна я в цім краю безлюднім,

на тебе все чекаючи з пустельними піснями.
О, моя шафранова любове, убрана в срібло
і в стрічки синьо-золоті!
Не маю я і гадки, сталось як, що наші ці стежки
переплелися і як ми для любові тут зустрілися.

* *Араваллі — гірський хребет у Раджастані, Індія, вважається найдавнішим у світі гірським утворенням.*

## The Day Death is Imminent

The day death is imminent, call me,
and I will meet you in no man's land.

I want to kiss the lips that spoke my name to the world and
the lines on the palms of your hands that wrote my destiny.

I will shield you with the parasol of my poetry.
I will make love to you, my warrior.

And make you immortal.

## День смерті неминучий все ж

День смерті неминучий все ж, мене поклич
і я знайду тебе в безлюднім краї.

Уста, що світові моє ім'я назвали, бажаю цілувати,
й долоні рук, якими написав мій чин, також бажаю.

Я захищу тебе покровом з моїх віршів.
Я буду тебе, воїне, любити.

І я зроблю тебе безсмертним.

# My Love is Not an Apology

If I must die
I wish to die
a happy death,
with a smile on my lips.

I wouldn't go confessing
anything to anyone.
My joy isn't a sin,
my love is not an apology!

# Моє кохання – не виправдання

Як я маю померти,
хочу померти
смертю легкою,
з усміхом на устах.

І мені сповідатися
немає ні в чому.
Моя втіха — не гріх,
а кохання — не виправдання!

## The Healer

Don't leave!
Stay. Speak to me.
Or the night—
won't progress.
The dawn won't break.
The moon, the stars,
and the night sky
wait in anticipation of
what you have to say,

what you are supposed to say,
what you must say,
no matter how difficult,
it won't break my heart.
Nothing can be broken
over again, but can mend.

And I don't care,
if I know your tongue,
or understand a word you say.
I just want to hear you speak,
like the wind is whispering in the canyon,
like a night bird singing to the moon,
like the sounds of the ocean waves
comforting the shore.
Nothing more, and never less.

## Цілитель

Не йди!
Зостанься. Розмовляй зі мною.
Інакше ніч
тягтиметься без краю.
Зоря не зійде.
Зірки і місяць,
небо ночі —
усе з надією в чеканні
на те, сказати маєш що,

на те, що міг сказати б,
на те, сказати мусиш що,
хай як там важко буде,
та серце не розіб'ється.
Ніщо зламать не можна
знову — поправити лише.

Не переймалась я б,
коли б знаття твоєї мови
чи розуміння слів хоча б.
Та серце вже не розіб'ється.
мов вітру шепіт у каньйоні,
мов птахи спів вночі до місяця,
мов океану звуки в хвилях,
що пестять берег.
Не більше і не менше.

## You and Me

I have walked in the gardens
void of fragrance for so long
to appreciate the wild blossom you are.

## Ти і я

Я прогулювалася у садах,
не просяклих пахощами, довго так,
аби оцінити цвіт дикий, яким ти є.

# God Doesn't Command Love

I welcome you as the earth welcomes
the sun, just to be there every day
and watch the miracles unfold.

The singing of the birds won't fill
the void of the sky if the sun won't rise,
sunflowers fields will wither,

the trees won't grow fruits,
rain won't return to the earth,
farmers won't sow seeds in their fields,

a river won't sparkle, ships won't sail,
night shelling won't stop, and the vampires
won't end their cravings for our blood.

There is a reason why the earth needs
the sun, no matter how far the distance.
There is no contract between them.

God doesn't command their love.
Yet, they are there for each other,
for the sake of the universe.

## Любити Творець не наказує

Я вітаю тебе, як земля — сонце,
просто за те, що це є щодня,
як і дива, що побачити можна.

Щебіт птахів небес порожнечу
не зможе заповнити, в разі, якщо
сонце не зійде, то сонях зів'яне,

дерева не будуть давати плодів,
дощі не кропитимуть землю, а фермери
не будуть її засівати насінням,

ріка не сіятиме, кораблі не ходитимуть,
обстріли нічні не припиняться, а
вампіри і далі смоктатимуть кров.

Єдина причина, чому потребує
сонця земля, незалежно від відстані, —
між ними ж угоди немає зовсім,

любити Творець не наказує їм, —
вони є залежні
заради усесвіту.

## A Lotus in the Autumn Garden

We didn't create a past of wrongdoings.
Nor should we anticipate a future
that will never arrive. Our souls must be free
from doubts and fear of the unknown.

All we have is the present moment,
blooming like a lotus in its purity
in our Autumn garden. Its delicate scent,
a rare invitation to rise in awareness.

Let's not close our eyes or look away!
Let's watch this miracle happening
even on a day when our pond is tinted with blood,
and its swamp can swallow us, if we ever make

the mistake of stepping into it.

## *Лотос в осінньому саду*

Ми не творили минулого з кривд.
І малювати майбутнє, яке не настане,
не маємо ми. Від сумнівів і переляку
перед незнаним хай звільняться душі

Єдине, що у нас — це мить тепер,
квітуча, наче лотос у саду осіннім
у чистоті. І ніжні пахощі його є дивним
запрошенням осяяння пізнати.

Тож не заплющуймо очей і не відводьмо!
Дивімося на диво, що стається,
навіть у день, коли наш став залитий кров'ю
і ця драгва спроможна нас поглинути, якщо колись

ми похитнемося, ступивши в нього.

## Love: This One Word

*~ A response to #BuchaMassacre, a poem by Ella Yevtushenko*

Love,
this one word
can change the entire world.

If their hearts were filled with love,
they would not have been tempted
to empty themselves in the bodies of women.

If love was sown as a seed
in the heart of your enemy, dear Ukraine,
it could have prevented Bucha from happening.

If love was planted in the gardens
by mothers, where their children played,
it could have saved women from dying with

their mouths filled with sand; those who sang
lullabies to their children and read them the stories
of their glorious land before being raped.

If the thread of love was tied as a wristband by girls
on their boys' hands before sending them to battlefields,
it could have prevented women from assaults in Bucha and

being thrown on the streets, undignified,
rolled in carpets, face down,
after being shot in their heads.

My warrior, my friend,
before you return to the battlefield again,
I want to fill every atom of your body with love.

And lace your breaths with the perfume of
my undying passion for your country to kiss
goodbye to you.

To prepare for war and to prevent another Bucha
from happening in any other corner of the earth,
we must be madly in love.

## Любов: однісінькe слово

*на поезію Елли Євтушенко «#BuchaMassacre»*

Любов,
однісіньке слово,
спроможне змінити весь світ.

Якби їх серця сповняла любов,
не спокусились вони б
себе спорожнити в жіночих тілах.

Якби насіниною в серці
твого ворога, дорога Україно, стала любов,
вона б стримала їх від Бучі.

Якби у всіх парках, де граються діти,
плекали любов матері,
це вберегло б від кончини жінок

із піском у їхніх горлянках: усіх, хто співав
колискові малятам, усіх, хто про землю славетну
билини розказував перед тим, як ґвалту зазнати.

Якби стрічку любові на юначі зап'ястя дівчата
пов'язали, як тих відсилають на фронт,
то тоді берегині не знали б навали на Бучу,

просто неба не кинули б їх на наругу,
долілиць, загорнутих у килими
після пострілу в голову.

Мій воїне, мій побратиме,
перед тим, як поїдеш ти знову на фронт,
я любов'ю сповни́ти бажаю твого тіла кожну клітинку

і скріпити твій дух ароматом
безсмертної пристрасті щодо твоєї країни,
поцілунок піднісши прощальний.

Аби до війни нам готовими бути і запобігти
Бучі подібній по цілому світу,
любити сповна ми повинні.

## A Bird of a Rare Species

The rules set for us by the world,
we follow them, only to break
every rule when we get a chance.

I have freed myself from the farce of
how the world defines love in the book of
morality to create a world so loveless.

Cut down your shackles, and break free
from the cage to fly in the endless sky
like a bird of a rare species.

Dance like a peacock in the garden of love
without a beloved. Not worrying about
saving the world but yourself.

## Рідкісний птах

Світом встановленим правилам
ми слідуємо, щоб порушити
перше ж правило, щойно дістанемо шанс.

Я звільнилась від фарсу, коли
світ визначає любов у книзі моралі,
щоб зробити його безлюбовним настільки.

Розірви свої пута, із кліті звільнись,
щоб злетіти у небо безкрає
тим рідкісним птахом.

Танцюй, наче павич, в любові садах
без коханої. Про рятунок турбуйся
не світу, а свій.

## The Conquest

And there is nothing wrong with
having aspirations for victory.
You wanted to win, so you must.
Your claim is just. Nevertheless,

O the defender of your land!
I wish you can understand
how wonderful it is to lose
the battles of passion to win
a war fought for love.

A face that you once envied,
the face that was nothing but
a reflection of yourself became
the pursuit of your heart and
a piece of art you must possess.

She wasn't aware of it,
she had no way of knowing
you felt defeated in
the failed conquest of your dreams,
so, you must conquer her soul,

to redeem your losses, as though
her heart was the only way to triumph over
the victory she had on your land. One way
or the other, you wanted that glory for yourself.
She doesn't reproach your approach.

No one wants to be defeated on his soil.
What right she had to enter—
the territories of the land you worshiped
to rule the hearts of your people?
The victory must be yours.

Your confession is laudable.
Your confidence is charming.
If you can't win, you must have
the heart of the reigning queen.

## Завоювання

У прагненні перемогти
немає злого аніскільки.
Ти прагнув перемог, отож здобудеш їх.
Такий закон. Але однак,

о оборонцю краю, я бажаю,
щоб ти збагнути зміг,
програти як чудово
в двобоях пристрасті, аби перемогти
у війнах за любов.

Особа, що їй заздрив ти,
оця особа, що була нічим —
лиш відбиттям твоїм, — сьогодні стала
полоном твого серця і мистецтва
творінням, яким оволодіти мусиш.

Твій намір невідомим був
для неї — не могла і знати
вона, що в змагу мрії
своєї ти прогрáєш,
тож її душу мусиш підкорити —

підсолодити гіркоту поразки, —
тріумф над серцем — це єдиний спосіб
перемогти звитяжця на твоїй землі.
Чи так, а чи інак хотів ти слави.
Тобі вона не докоряє.

Ніхто програти на своїй землі не хоче.
Кому хто право дав ввійти
у край, якому поклонявся ти,
аби серцями володіти?
Твоєю мусить бути перемога.

Шляхетним є твоє зізнання.
Чарує впевненість твоя.
Коли перемогти не можеш,
пануй у серці королеви.

## Valor

There is much valor in the defeat of
a warrior on the battlegrounds of love.

The triumphant returns home
with a broken heart.

## Доблесть

Є так багато доблесті у воїнській поразці,
на теренах боїв любові.

Звитяжець повертається
з розбитим серцем.

## War at 7-Eleven

A guy at the 7-Eleven gas station
looked at me and said, *you look happy.*
*Didn't you check the gas prices?*
*The war, man! This war!*
*It is killing us.* He went on...

*Food, gas, clothing,*
*you can't afford anything!*
His words bore truth.
I felt sad and thought—

is there any way to lure the beast,
sitting at your door, put him into a cage,
carry him on your tank
and let him loose in a forest,
even animals have abandoned?

## Війна на заправці

Хлопчина на заправці «Севен елевен»
подивився на мене і сказав: «Ви — щасливі!
Ви не зауважили нової ціни!
Людино, війна! Війна ось!
Вона нас вбиває, — і відійшов… —

Від палива, їжі, одежі
не зможеш відгородитись ніяк!»
Від слів цих дошкульних
у смутку, задумалась я:

«Чи існує приманка для звіра,
який оббиває пороги твої, щоб у кліті
на танку його відвезти
та кинути в лісі,
з якого і звірі втекли?»

## Slava Ukraini!

The hope in me is you.
Even in the darkest times,
the peace in me is you,
the light in me is you.

But you are restless.

You hold the charging handle of your machine gun
and wish there was no one between your bullets
and the world you have fallen in love with,
but it's too late.

Your enemy has chosen its destiny, and so have you.

Allow your motherland to accept their dead bodies,
break them down into atoms, and someday
grow them as the lovers of your land.
No matter what the world says—

You carry your cross and talk peace, even when no one is listening.

One must die, for the truth to be resurrected.
But the bridge of hope and trust before you is broken,
and you wander like a dog, loyal and forlorn,
on the ravished grounds of your motherland,

licking her wounds, feeling her pain...

A faint smoke rises, from the fire lit before you,
your faith alive in its dying ashes. With bare hands,
you salvage the songs of Psalms under the burnt bridge and
make a promise to your motherland—to retain her honor.

"Slava Ukraini! Glory to mother Ukraine!"

## Слава Україні!

В мені надія — ти.
І в темряви часи
мир у мені — це ти,
і світло — також ти.

Та сам-самісінький ти неспокійний.

Заряджений стискаєш автомат
з одним бажанням: поміж кулями і світом —
у нім ти так невчасно покохав — щоб не було нікого,
та надто пізно.

Обрав твій ворог долю вже таку, тому й ти теж.

Дозволь вже Батьківщині поховати своїх героїв,
що на атоми розпалися, тому колись
постануть з них мужі любові землі твоєї.
І хай що світ говорить —

Несеш ти хрест і слово миру, хай не почуте ще ніким в ці дні.

Комусь за правду вмерти доведеться, аби воскреснути.
Та міст надій і віри розбили ще раніше,
тому блукаєш, мов собака вірний, безпритульний
на землях поґвалтованих твоєї Батьківщини,

сповнившись болем, рани зализавши не всі…

Ледь-ледь димить вогонь перед тобою.
У попелі твоя посвята є живою. І під мостом,
що спалений, ти голіруч псалми спасаєш
і присягаєш Батьківщині — гідність вберегти їй.

«Вкраїні — слава! Слава Україні-матері!»

## Dear Ukraine, Merry Christmas!

The tenacity of humanity is not in attaining
what cannot be granted as an act of mercy.

Instead, it is to accept what we have been deprived of
with utmost dignity, only to have the aspiration for

the freedom we must have and to make
all that is denied possible for us.

Once, a statue of the Buddha was erected in a monastery
with the bullet casings left behind by soldiers.

The mountains of Escondido, filled with the smell of
gunpowder were purified with the perfume of pure land.

The rocks sprouted trees from their hearts and
animals and birds returned home to sing and dream.

Today, Ukraine has a Christmas tree made with
camouflage nets in Mykolaiv, with a star of hope,

and ornaments of dreams, blue and yellow.
Like a dove with an olive branch in its beak—

Kyiv waits for Santa to arrive,
dodging missiles and drone strikes.

The snow keeps carrots and milk from spoiling
for reindeer arriving in Odesa—without power and water.

You see, the enemy can destroy all but
the hopes and dreams in the eyes of Ukraine.

Her children are invincible. They are dreaming of Christmas,
baking loaves of bread and cookies for Santa,

who is serving on their frontiers, dressed like a warrior,
hidden in every soldier, committed to delivering,

the gift of their dream—their freedom.
Merry Christmas, dear Ukraine! And a Happy New Year in glory!

## Дорога Вкраїно, Христа славімо!

Людські вічні клопоти — не заради досягнень
чогось, що не стане дарунком від щирого серця.

Це значить, усе слід прийняти, чого нас позбавили,
із гідністю справжньою, аби тільки мати

до волі стремління, що мусимо мати,
щоб втілити все, у чому відмовлено нам.

Статую Будди в одному із монастирів вирізьбили з
відстріляних гільз, що їх залишили солдати.

Гори Ескондідо, раніше просякнуті порохом,
стали омитими чистих земель ароматами.

Скелі проросли деревами з їхніх сердець,
а звір і птахи повернулись додому співати і мріяти.

Днесь в Україні — різдвяна ялинка із камуфляжних
сіток в Миколаєві, із зорею надії

на вершику та витинанками мрій, синьо-жовтих.
Неначе той голуб з оливковим листям у дзьобі,

очікує Київ, прийде як святий Миколай,
від дронів, крилатих ракет ухилившись.

Сніги не дають зіпсуватися моркві й молочному —
в Одесу без світла й води олені все ж добираються.

Під силу, мабуть, усе знищити ворогу,
окрім — це всім ясно — мрій і надій України.

Непереможні тут діти — щасливого всім Різдва
побажають і коржики для Миколая святого

спечуть, бо служить він в однострої,
десь там, де лінія фронту, вселившись у кожного воїна,

який у дарунок приносить омріяне — волю!
Славімо Христа, Україно! І славного Нового року!

## War at Five

For you, it was just another air raid siren,
another day at the war. For me,
like the end of the world for a moment...

The last time I heard an air raid siren, I was five.
Eating dinner in my courtyard. I had to leave my plate
for the moon. The lights went off.

Eleven Indian airbases were bombed.
I was tucked into my blanket alone.
No one to explain to me what war does.

I had no one to ask for a song.
I had to imagine everything.
I continue to imagine everything.

I am glad, this time, you were there.
I am glad our songs could save us
through the night—rescued by the morning.

## Війна, коли лише п'ять

Для тебе — це просто знову сирени
і ще один день із війни. А для мене —
це світу кінець наче ось вже настав...

Востаннє я чула сирену в п'ять років.
Не доївши обіду надворі, тарілку
залишила для місяця. Світло вимкнулось.

Індійські авіабази, всі одинадцять, бомбили.
Закутана в ковдру свою, я стояла сама.
І ніхто не спромігся сказати мені: почалася війна.

Я нікого не мала, аби попросити про пісню.
Я мала лише уявляти усе.
І далі я все уявляю.

Я радію, що ти цього разу був поруч.
Я радію, що наші пісні уночі
нас змогли врятувати — й на ранок ми були живі.

** Під час Третьої індо-пакистанської війни 3 грудня 1971 року авіація Повітряних сил Пакистану завдала повітряного удару по індійських військових аеродромах.*

## War and Flowers

The flowers did not go to the weddings and birthdays as planned,
the christenings of the newborns, or to profess love for valentines.
They did not sit at homes in vases. They refused to go
to the palaces of dictators and monarchs.

They did not go to the temples, churches and synagogues,
or offer themselves to God and Godmen.
They went to honor the coffins of the soldiers
and unmarked graves of the brave and innocents.

They traveled to the borders to welcome refugees
and sat on shrines to pray for peace.
And before they wilted in fire and snow,
the flowers scattered their seeds to regrow.

Everyone takes a new role in a war.

# Війна і квіти

Квіти, усупереч планам, не йшли на весілля і дні
народження, на хрестини і для валентинок,
не сиділи і вдома у вазах, йти відмовились до
палаців диктаторів і самодержців.

Вони і не йшли до церков, синагог і осель для моління,
на пожертви Творцеві і пожертви святим,
а пішли вшанувати воїнів труни й
безіменні могили хоробрих, невинних.

Вони — до кордонів для зустрічі біженців
і — на святині — молитись за мир.
І, перш ніж зів'янути в полум'ї й снігові,
насіння своє розкидáли, щоб вирости ще.

У кожного роль нова за часів війни.

## Good Company

Among many faces of the war
is a beautiful kitten. Lost
or abandoned, you can't tell.

Somehow she had gotten under a hanger
with the soldiers on a command post of
the Ukrainian Armed Forces in Mariupol.

She sits by the stove for warmth
and looks at him as I would
when he mixes his coffee.

And I know my soldier is
in good company.

## Добра компанія

Поміж образків багатьох з війни
є і миле кошеня. Загубилося
чи покинули, не дізнатися.

Дивом воно прибилося до
ангару з оборонцями
на командному пункті ЗСУ в Маріуполі.

Біля буржуйки сидить, гріється
і дивиться на нього так, як і я,
коли він заварює каву.

І знаю, що мій воїн —
у добрій компанії.

## Puppies at the Base

The newborn puppies,
on a military base are learning
how to grind axes, how to chop wood.

They are learning how to count the bodies,
and discover graves, looking for
their missing father and mother.

They run up and down the stump of a tree anxiously.
There is no warm milk of their mother's breast.
Among your sacrifices, you make sure their losses count.

# Цуцики на вопі*

Новонароджені цуцики
на маленькому вопі навчаються,
як гострити сокири, як колоти дрова.

Вони навчаються, підрахувати тіла як
і як знайти поховання, шукаючи
ненька і неньку, яких загубили.

Вони метушливо застрибують на колоду і зістрибують з неї.
Немає теплого молока із сосків нені.
Поміж усіх жертв ти упевнишся: їх втрати підраховані.

** Воп — взводний опорний пункт, елемент бойового порядку військового формування в зоні ведення бойових дій.*

## Children of Earth

Bridges came down, and rivers flooded.
Hundreds and thousands of acres of forests were destroyed.*
Where did the animals go for refuge?
Where did the birds go to nest?

Would the pelicans return in Spring to their water,
to see the cetaceans dead on their seabeds?

They shot dogs on the streets and ate them on the eastern front.
Would that be considered a war crime? Who will determine
the losses and compensation for the children of the earth?
Would they ever be heard and reimbursed rightly?

**Some seven hundred thousand acres of forests have been destroyed in the current Russia-Ukrainian war.*

## Діти Землі

Впали мости і ріки розлилися.
Знищено сотні тисяч гектарів угідь і лісів*.
Звірам де притулок шукати?
Птахам де гніздуватись тепер?

Чи повернуться пелікани навесні,
аби побачити дельфінів мертвих на морському дні?

Відстріляли на вулицях псів і з'їли на східному фронті
Чи військовим злочином це назовуть? І кому визначати
втрати і компенсації дітям землі?
Чи почують колись їх і чи належно усе відшкодують?

** За даними Всесвітнього фонду природи, внаслідок війни в Україні знищено 700 000 акрів лісу, або 280 000 гектарів (28 000 кв. км).*

## The New Year's Eve

It hasn't been a good day.

But why should I expect every day
to be as good as our conversations
in the darkest of times, amidst the sounds
of shutter clicks, of your machine guns
echoing in the realms of your forests, villages,
towns, and the chambers of your heart
that draw you near me, and we sit across
from each other on the tables of our continents
to have tea together, holding our empty cups
to be filled with grace, listening to silence
that holds all meanings?

Why should I expect my noon to be
full of laughter, on your naivety
about my ability to handle doubts and fears
when the noises of your cannons are loud
in your steppes, and the ominous sounds of
sirens run across your streets, robbing your nation
of the hope for peace, and all that matters to you,
and we don't speak for days, quietened with chaos?

How can I ask my evenings to be warm
when you stand in the face of raging snow storms
on your frontiers to ensure your country's freedom?
Flung across oceans that divide our lands,
I do not know—where you are tonight.
What code of intelligence you are writing,
without pen and paper, electricity, and
electronic devices to talk to God, to take the Devil
back to his workshop and rewire his brain at once?

We did not kiss in Time Square, New York,
when the clock folded its hands at midnight,
ushering us into a new year. Our glasses
didn't fill with champagne, but rage and tears.
And we held them tight, preventing a single drop
from spilling, as it would have forever flooded the earth.

There was no Christmas in your trenches, dear Ukraine.
Santa wore camouflage and gave his robe back to God in protest.

There was no celebration of the new year in your snowfields
dotted with blood. But we have another day of sunshine,
the saplings of hope in our roots, and flower buds
in the branches of our bones waiting for Spring.
We have another night, brightened with the milk
of the moonlight. And that's all matters!

## Новорічна ніч

День виявився недобрим.

Та навіщо чекати, щоб він
добрим був, як і (наче) наші розмови
в найтемніші часи, серед ляскання
затворів твоїх автоматів,
що відлунюють у лісах, у містах,
у хатах і у закутках серця твого,
що тебе прикликує, і навпроти один одного
ми всідаємось по своїх континентах
чаювати разом, з порожніми чашками,
аби благодаттю наповнюватися, тишу
слухаючи, у якій — найцінніше і справжнє?

Та чому сподіватися маю, щоб моє пообіддя
сповнялося сміхом, оскільки ти віриш наївно
щодо спромоги моєї здолати всі сумніви
і страхи, коли твої гаубиці — в реві гучнім
у степах і завивання зловісне сирен
по вулицях котиться, викрадаючи в нації
надію на мир і на все, що істотне для тебе,
а ми — без розмов цілі дні, затихлі у хаóсі?

Просити як мені про теплі вечори,
коли шторми зимові, люті обличчям зустрічаєш ти
на кордонах, щоб забезпечити свободу краю?
Закинута за океани, що ділять землі наші,
я не знаю, де застане тебе ніч сьогодні.
Який розвідувальний код ти твориш
без ручки та листка, електрики й девайсів,
щоб поговорити з Богом і повернути
диявола назад до пекла, аби перепрошити йому мізки?

В нью-йоркському Тайм-сквері не цілувались ми,
коли годинник північ відбивав,
у новий рік нас переводячи. І склянки наші
не шампанським, а люттю і слізьми наповнені.
І ми тримали міцно їх, щоб жодна крапля
не розлилася, бо це б залило землю навіки.

Різдва не було, дорога Україно, в окопах твоїх.
Архистратиг — у камуфляжі нині, віддавши Богу плащ.

Новорічних гулянь не було у замерзлих полях,
кров'ю зрошених. …А у нас — ще один сонячний день,
надії ростки із коріння у нас і квіткова брость
на вітті наших кісток на весну чекають.
У нас ще одна ніч, освітлена місячним
сяйвом. І в цьому є сенс!

## For the Sons of the Kyivan Rus

Although my songs for you are
like the songs of *Meera,*
I would rather be your *Mastani* in Bakhmut any day.

Evil will never go down in history as a hero.
O *Bajirao,* of the Kyivan Rus, it has to be you
in silver, yellow and blue.

*Meera—A Rajput princess who loved Krishna and wrote devotional songs for him.*

*Mastani—A Rajput-Muslim princess who loved the Peshwa Ruler, Bajirao, and fought battles together with him against the Mughal invasion of India.*

## Синам Київської Русі

Хоча мої пісні для тебе є
піснями Міри* наче,
та кращев Бахмуті Мастані** буду я колись твоєю.

Ніколи зло героєм у історію не ввійде.
О Баджі Рао Київської Русі, це — ти
у сріблі, жовтому та синьому.

** Міра — раджпутська принцеса, яка любила Крішну і писала для нього релігійні пісні.*

*** Мастані (1699—1740) — індійська (браджпутська) принцеса, друга дружина Баджі Рао I, пешви, правителя маратхів, поруч з яким воювала проти Великих Моголів, які кілька століть прагнули підкорити Індію.*

# Coming Home

I

Away from dark waters,
let's step into the warm currents of
the ocean now, where our spirits can sparkle

without any residue of
the unpleasant past, to have a future
for the rare bond, we have created through
our bravery and creativity, and
the generosity of our hearts toward others.

Let's allow our sorrows to sleep and joy to be awakened.
We yet have to return to our *true home.* *
We yet have to call each other by our *true names*.**

*"Your True Home," by Thich Nhat Hanh (2011)
***"Call Me By My True Names," by Thich Nhat Hanh (1993)*

## Повернення додому

I

Тепер нам час зробити крок
у теплі води океану від темних течій якнайдалі —
дух кожного тоді засяє

без осаду з минулих днів,
ганебних днів, аби майбутнє
в єднанні неповторному плекати —
його створили ми в сердець глибинах,
щедротами і творчістю скріпивши.

Тож смуток хай засне, щоб пробудилась радість.
Нам слід ще повернутись до правдивої домівки.
Нам слід ще відзиватися на справжні імена свої.

* *Тхіть Ньят Хань, «Твій справжній дім» (2011, англ.)*
* *Тхіть Ньят Хань, «Називай мене справжніми іменами» (1993)*

## Coming Home

II

On your shoulders you carry
the burdens of your grieving nation.
And I carry you in my heart
for you to unburden yourself.
In the process, we become
an ocean for each other, where
we end our journey like a river
to return to our forever home.

## Повернення додому

### II

На плечах несеш тягар
скорботної нації своєї.
А я несу у серці тебе,
щоб розвантажити.
Поступово стаємо ми
океаном один для одного,
закінчуючи подорож, наче ріка,
аби повернутись до вічного прихистку.

## The Sand in Our Eyes

The sand in our eyes this morning is
from the river that has flown
in our hearts all night.

A river has a destiny of its own.
It can wash off the sins of anyone

but is always left with a swamp within,
whether that is Ganges or Dnipro,
Indus or Tigris, Perfume or Delaware.

O my warriors! The story is the same!
The sand in our eyes—in flames!

## Пісок в очах у нас

Пісок в очах у нас сьогодні вранці —
з річки, яка текла
в серцях всю ніч.

Ріка несе покликання для нас.
Вона гріхи усі спроможна змити,

проте в заплавах залишається завжди́,
байдуже Ґанґ це, Інд, а чи Дніпро,
Хионґ, чи Тигр, чи Делавер.

О мій воїне! Історія завжди́ та сама.
Пісок в очах у нас — горить!

## A Year of The War

I

It has been almost a year of the war.
We have lost the concept of time.
We have adjusted our body clocks
and turned around seasons in our minds
to live—not merely survive.

We have manifested the sun at night—
without light. We have plucked the moon in a panic
to cover it in shelter, from the eyes of sky pirates.
There is chaos in every vein of Ukraine.
Peace has gone missing in the terrain.

Doubt and uncertainties are in the air.
But somewhere, there is a willingness
to make things work,
everything that is broken.
Everything that has been broken!

# Рік війни

I

Минув ще один рік війни.
Ми загубили часу відчуття,
і тіл годинники перелаштували,
і пори року у думках змінили
на те, щоб жити, а не виживати.

Ми виявили сонце серед ночі—
без світла. Ми місяць в паніці зірвали,
щоб в укритті його сховати від очей повітряних піратів.
У кожній вені України — хáос.
І спокій зник у краю цім.

В повітрі — сумнів і непевність.
Але між тим живе бажання —
хай все працює,
усе поламане.
Усе поламане!

## Bakhmut

Dear sweet land, take me to where you hurt most.
And the sun came down from the sky to be my tour guide.
It showed me the darkest of wounds in Bucha, Mariupol, Soledar,
and Dnipro, with the help of its flashlight, shaking in its hand.
It took me to Bakhmut, abandoned by fear.

On its way, it grabbed a loaf of bread from a shelter
for the citizens who wouldn't surrender their city.
It took me to every alley and street in the town,
pounded by armored vehicles, tanks, and boots on the ground.
Bodies of soldiers without souls and angels with broken wings,
littered everywhere. Countless dead defending their paradise.

*Bakhmut holds!* The ice patches along the road heal
the bruises of the city from yesterday's battle.
At noon, we sat on a bench for poetry in a decimated park.
It chewed on the pieces of bread without butter,
shared a piece with me, and bits with the birds
gathered for crumbs and the rare presence of humans.

The sun looked old, very old. Its eyes glowed
in the volleys of fire from every war it witnessed
in its lifetime. Its lips parched from the flames
of a river it drank after lunch. And in its wrinkle folds,
it hid all its sorrows to save my trust in humanity.

# Бахмут

Мила земле, візьми ось мене у місця, найболючіші нині.
І спустилося сонце, аби мені шлях показати.
Й посвітило на — чорніших немає — в Маріуполі, Бучі, Дніпрі, Соледарі
ліхтарем у тремтячій руці.
І привело мене в Бахмут, покинутий страхом.

По дорозі схопило хлібину зі сховку
для тих городян, що міста вони не здадуть.
І мене привело у кожен провулок і вулицю міста,
розтрощені танками і БМП, зачовгані сірим взуттям.
Солдатські тіла вже без душ і без ангелів з крилами зламаними
повсюдно лежать. Без числа полягли, захищаючи рай.

*Бахмут тримається!* Приморозь побіч дороги
гоїть місту синці після вчорашніх боїв.
В полудень сіли на лавці для віршів у знищенім парку.
Сонце жувало розламаний хліб без нічого
і зі мною шматком поділилось, а іншим — з птахами —
злетілись на крихти і заради присутніх, що рідкість, людей.

Сонце старим виглядало, аж надто. І сяяли очі його
у залпах гарматних тих воєн, що бачило
у плині свойого життя. Пересохли вже губи
від полум’я річки, що випило у пообіддя. І в зморшках
воно приховало весь сум, щоб у людяність віру мою зберегти.

## Soledar

I offer water and tea at the altar
to spiritual and blood ancestors,
and call upon them to ease the sufferings of the universe.

I know my prayer reaches them as you have a way of
reaching me through unknown channels that can't be seen
through the naked eye, or technology in the sky.

But unlike me, you wouldn't admit when you hurt.
I have to figure this out myself. And today, it's Soledar,
and the absence of your martyred children, the salt of their nation.

There may not be any walls left standing in your city,
but you have your foundations, the fundamentals,
the grounds you stand on in your offensive.

And that matters before denying victory to you
in your holy war. They must go back after
picking up the corpses of their sons, in vain.

There is so much hurt in burying them
in your heart, dear Ukraine!

# Соледар

Я приношу чай і воду на вівтар
духовним, кровним предкам — закликаю їх
полегшити страждання світу.

Я знаю: ці прохання їм приходять, бо і тобі до мене
відомий шлях крізь сховані канали, які ніколи
ні оком неозброєним, ні технікою в небі не побачити.

Як я, не дієш ти — ти б не зізнався, коли болить.
Я маю з'ясувати це сама. І нині — Соледар,
твоїх замучених дітей, які є сіллю нації, відсутність.

Мабуть, ніяких стін у місті не лишилось,
однак у тебе є твої основи та підстави,
той ґрунт, стоїш на ньому що заради наступу.

І буде так наперекір невірі у твою звитягу
в священній цій війні. Вони відступлять неодмінно,
намарне підбираючи тіла своїх синів.

І скільки болю в тім, що їх усіх ховаєш
у своїм серці, милий Краю!

# Paradise Lost

There is a myth about us.
Then there is reality.
I want you to know
the real me.

The day you think
you have known me,
you stop knowing me,
as I am constant, flowing—

like the stream which carries me
to the unchartered lands,
that has brought me to you,
dear Ukraine,

and I stand with you
in the rubble of Dnipro
with cracks in our hearts,
yet unbroken!

Let's not cast doubts about
why I am here. Who am I?
I am here at your invitation.
We are in this hell together!

Searching for our paradise lost.

## Утрачений рай

Про нас є міт.
Та є і дійсність.
Бажаю я, щоб ти пізнав
мене правдиву.

Як лиш подумаєш,
що знаєш,
тобі я стану невідомою,
бо — стала я

мов той потік, який мене
несе в непізнані краї,
який до тебе донесе,
о Краю милий,

і я стою з тобою тут
на пагорбах крутих Дніпра,
і тріщини в серцях у нас.
Та я не зламана!

Тож сумніви женімо геть
у тім, чому я тут і ким я є.
Я — на запрошення твоє.
В цім пеклі разом ми!

Шукаючи *утрачений рай.*

# A Year of the War

II

You see, it has been a year,
but the war has not ended.
In fact, it has been
more than a year!
Nine years to be precise.
Or perhaps longer,
if we dig a little deeper.

We hope the conflict ends soon.
Sooner than our tanks arrive
at their comfortable pace
at your frontiers, before
the Wings of Freedom descend
from the skies, like angels.

Before Oranta cries one last time
against the immovable wall of
your heavy heart—
under the layer of your shirt,
my eyelashes can still touch
from an immeasurable distance.

We hope for the war to end soon.
Sooner than the world expects,
sooner than you promise yourself
to avenge the death of your knights,
vowing on your fifth commandment.*

But it's not always what we want.
Wars never end.
We take our battles home.
They are camouflaged into our hearts.
We fight more fiercely than ever.
We bleed more profusely.

We sacrifice the best years of our lives
thinking about the wars we have fought,
counting the days and years of faded hopes,
the numbers of our battles,
detesting our enemies every day,

searching in rubble our lost homes,
the faces we loved lost in clouds.

We dig trenches in our souls and
stay there for life. Until the last day.
The enemy within occupies
every inch of our souls,
forcing us into exile.
And no nation willing to take us.

Many of us die in oblivion,
crossing deserts, in valleys of death,
on the borders of foreign lands.
But someday, the war will be over,
and the sun will take out its victory chariot
for you to ride, and circle the earth.

I know you will fight till the end—
for this day to arrive in your promised land.
And for every drop of blood—
shed on your battlefields,
every bead of sweat on your forehead,
I, too, shall write a love song till the end.

**The fifth point of the "Ten Commandments of the Ukrainian Nationalists."*

# Рік війни

II

Вже рік війни минув,
та їй кінця не видно.
Триває більше року,
по суті, ця війна!
Точніше — дев'ять літ.
Ба навіть довше,
заглибитись коли.

В надії ми — кінець конфлікту прийде.
Вже скоро. Від танків наших швидше,
що прибувають у зручно́му темпі
до вас на фронт, від крил свободи
раніше, ніж опустяться вони
з небес подібно ангелам.

До миті як Оранта востаннє скрикне
навпроти непорушної стіни
твого важкого серця
під полотном сорочки
я віями торкнутись зможу ще
із відстані незміряної.

В надії ми — кінець війні настане.
Вже скоро. Від очікування світу швидше,
від сповнення обітниці помститися
за смерть великих лицарів,
як сказано у п'ятій точці*, швидше.

Однак не те стається, що бажаємо.
Кінця немає війнам.
Свої бої додому забираємо,
закамуфльовані в серцях.
Затятіше ми не боролись.
Сильніше не кровило нам.

В офіру — час найкращий наш,
коли про війни, у яких боролись, мислимо,
рахуючи роки і дні погаслих сподівань,
численні битви,
ненавидячи ворогів щоденно,

шукаючи в руїнах втрачені домівки й
обличчя, що любили ми, загублені у хмарах.

Окопи в душах наших вириваємо, аби на
все життя вони зали́шились. До дня останнього.
А ворог із середини загарбує
за дюймом дюйм душ наших,
до втечі нас примушуючи.
І жодна нація приймати нас не хоче.

Багато з нас у забутті вмирають,
долаючи пустелі і долини смерті,
неподалік кордонів чужоземних.
Та все ж колись закі́нчиться війна,
а переможну колісницю сонечко подасть,
аби навкруг землі тобі зробити подорож.

Я знаю: до кінця виборювати будеш день,
який на ці благословенні землі прийде.
За кров усю, яку на бойовищах
пролито, і за кожну краплю поту,
який стікав з чола,
я допишу любовну пісню до кінця.

* *П'ята точка — п'ята заповідь Декалогу українського націоналіста.*

## Our Yellow Submarine

When you shared the story of the dead cetaceans
washed off the Black Sea shores, I saw you plunge
into the dark waters of your ocean to experience
its hidden trauma, from where I emerged for you.
You were the shell, and I was a pearl.

Taste my tears to know we were formed
in the same salt and water, and now dying
like sea mammals due to the acoustic trauma
caused by the sonar of our karmic chaos.

We didn't dream of our *Yellow Submarine** to see this day.
Did we? Let's not listen to the dreadful, deafening sounds.
Let's kiss and allow our breath to save the lives of each other.
Let's tell the enemies they are not welcome with their fleets
on the water we call our *True Home...* **

**Yellow Submarine, by The Beatles*
***Your True Home, by Thich Nhat Hanh*

## Наш човен жовтий *

Коли ти розповів історію про мертвих дельфіновидих,
змитих із чорноморських берегів, побачила я — ти пірнув
у темні води свого океану, аби зрозуміти
приховані травми, звідкіля я для тебе тільки постала.
Ти мушлею був, я — перлиною.

Мої сльози скуштуй, щоб дізнатись, що сіль і вода —
ті самі, з яких нас створили, і, наче кити чи дельфіни
з акустичними травмами від впливу сонару
кармічного хаосу нашого, нині миг инемо.

Не про це, щоб Човен наш жовтий зустрів цю хвилину, мріяли ми.
Так? Не слухаймо звуків страшних і оглушливих.
Цілуймось і диханню даймо життя нам з тобою спасти.
А недругам киньмо: їм, їхнім флотам тут не раді —
на водах нашого Справжнього дому**…

** Пісня «Бітлз» «Yellow Submarine».*
*** Тхіть Ньят Хань, «Твій справжній дім» (2011, англ.).*
*Тхіть Ньят Хань (1926–2022)— буддійський монах і вчитель, автор понад 100 книг, входив у сотню найвпливовіших духовних лідерів сучасності. Навчався в Колумбійському університеті, Прінстоні та Сорбонні, був номінований Мартіном Лютером Кінгом на Нобелівську премію миру. В'єтнамський уряд заборонив йому повертатися на батьківщину, тож він отримав політичний притулок у Франції.*

## Warriors: Bracing for War

He locked his heart and threw away the key.
And she opened to the core to let the world in.
He switched off the sound buttons to avoid distractions.
And she invited her bell to hear the silences speak.
He buzzed his head and put on his uniform. She took
a robe, and every lock of her hair fell into her lap.

Both bowed to each other before taking weapons.
In his hands is a machine gun to defend his nation.
In her hands is a double-edged sword to cut the illusion,
and rescue the souls wounded and lost.
He feeds himself a meal ready to eat. In her bowl—
there is nothing. She fasts. She is the last!*

He runs mile after mile to fuel his body, grieving his losses.
She stands solid on one leg with her arms up and palms joined,
like a lotus bud, her gaze pointed at the sun rising. He hears her
sing like a night bird in agony. And she watches him howl,
like a wounded wolf in his mountain looking at the moon.
He returns to his den wanting nothing in the end.

And she maps the cosmos to find their stars lost and stolen.
Both pray in their hearts—one to God—and one to—no one.

**Matthew 19:29-30.*

## Воїни: Підготовка до війни

Він серце своє замкнув і викинув ключ.
Вона своє серденя відчинила, світ щоб впустити.
Він звук сповіщення вимкнув, не відволікатися щоб.
Вона увімкнула дзвінок свій, щоб чути, як тиша говорить.
Він голову поголив і зодягнув однострій. А вона —
свій халат, і пасма волосся упали їй на коліна.

Одне одному перше, ніж зброю узяти, вклонились.
Автомат у нього в руках для захисту нації.
Меч двосічний у неї в руках, аби розрубати ілюзію
і врятувати душі, поранені і заблукалі.
Він їсть сухпайки. В її мисці нічого немає —
вона постить. Вона є «останньою»*!

Він довгі забіги долає, щоб тіло своє підживити, по втратах сумуючи.
Вона стоїть непохитно у позі дерева**, руки з'єднавши,
мов лотос в бутоні, із зором на сонце, що сходить. Він чує —
співає вона, мов пташина нічна, що страждає. Вона бачить —
він виє, наче поранений вовк, що до місяця тягнеться.
Він до лігва свого повертається, не бажаючи більше нічого.

Вона створює космосу карту, знайти щоб зірки їхні втрачені, вкрадені.
І молиться кожен: Творцеві — один, а інша — нікому.

** Єв. від Матвія 19:30.*
*** Поза дерева у йозі — на одній нозі, піднявши руки і з'єднавши долоні.*

## To Make Sure

Someday her five senses would dissolve in ether,
and she won't call. You will long to hear her words,
but she won't speak. She will return to where
she had come from without leaving a trace.
There won't be any footprints to track back.

You won't see the three dots pulsating on your phone,
on your messenger app, trying to cover a distance of
six thousand miles in one breath. That day—
the moon will be a total eclipse. The planets will go
retrograde, and the sun will begin to extinguish, bit by bit.

Someday your heart will be struck by a thunderbolt and
your outcry will rattle the earth and sky, but she won't return.
You will yearn for warmth, but she won't appear
in her *Pashmina,** woven with the yarns of her fragrant, tender
breath, with your name written on it, in its intricate patterns.

When the demon of destiny scoops your heart out mercilessly,
she will stop pulsing in the rivers of your veins.
The scent of her body permeated your pores and rubbed off
on your skin like saffron, the harvest of her sacred land,
will then return to her valleys, in defiance.

And you, like a musk deer, will search for the source of
her divine aroma in bewilderment, in forests,
not knowing she had been all along, within you.
You will run and run. The planet will heat up and burn.
But she will no longer return to fetch clouds and rain
for your combusting heart and lands in flames.

Your eyes will look for her in everyone you see,
everywhere you go, but you won't find glimpses of her
in the planet and her reflections in your waters.
She wouldn't appear on the screen of the sky.
The days will be darkened with the thick smoke of
lava oozing from your heart incessantly.

And even before you know it, the curtain from
the heavens will come down, and the show will end.
Loving until the last day, isn't for everyone.

It's a privilege granted to those who go last.
But you can't evade your destiny. And alas!

In the absence of love, Mariupol and Buccha
will happen again on this earth. Women will be taken
as prizes in wars. They will be raped and murdered
and there won't be enough sheets and carpets left
on the planet to cover their undignified bodies,

—before being tossed naked on their streets
in front of the eyes of their children after
one last bullet is pumped into their heads
just to make sure they are dead!
Just to make sure, love is dead forever!

**Pashmina refers to the Kashmiri Pashmina shawl made with cashmere wool, famous for its hand embroidery and softness.*

## Запевнитися

Якогось дня розчиняться в ефірі її п'ять почуттів
і не дзвонитиме вона. Захочеш ти її слова почути,
але вона не скаже їх. Мабуть, повернеться туди,
прийшла звідкіль, і сліду не лишивши.
І жодних зачіпок, аби її знайти, не буде.

Ти не побачиш крапок, які пульсують ні на смартфоні,
ні в месенджері, які здолати прагнуть відстань
в шість тисяч миль на подиху одному. І місячне
затемнення в той день у небі. Планети у зворотний бік
полинуть, стане й сонце гаснути поволі.

Якогось дня у серці ти відчуєш грім і
здригнуться небо і земля від твого крику, та вона не повернеться.
Ти будеш прагнути її тепла, але не з'явиться вона
в пашміні* з пряжі із її пахучих, ніжних подихів
з твоїм ім'ям, написаним на ній химерним візерунком.

Якщо черпатиме безжальний демон долі серце
твоє, вона не стане більше пульсувати в ріках вен твоїх.
І аромати її тіла, які ввібралися у шкіру
подібно до шафрану, її священної землі врожаю,
тоді повернуться в свої долини в непокорі.

І ти, мов кабарга, збентежений в лісах
шукатимеш джерел цих дивних пахощів її,
не знаючи: вона була в тобі весь час.
Ти будеш бігти, далі й далі. Земля нагрілася б, згоріла б.
Вже не повернеться вона, щоб дощ і хмари принести
в твоє сполум'яніле серце, на землі спалені.

У кожній жінці виглядатимеш її,
де б не пішов, але і відсвіту не знайдеш
на цій планеті, як і відбиття у ваших водах.
Не з'явиться вона й на небосхилі.
Затьмаряться густим туманом дні,
що з серця безупинно ллються лавою.

І ще до того, як помітиш це, завіса з неба
опуститься, завершивши виставу.
Кохання до останніх днів є не для всіх.
Це привілей лиш тих, хто йде останнім.
Однак від долі не втечеш, на жаль!

І без любові Маріуполь, Буча
повторяться. І братимуть жінок
як здобич на війні. Їх ґвалтуватимуть, вбиватимуть,
тканин і килимів не вистачатиме по всій планеті,
аби прикрити їх зневажені тіла,

і перед тим, як голими на вулиці
їх викинуть, а діти їх це будуть бачити,
останню кулю їм у голову засадять,
аби переконатися, що мертві!
Аби переконатись, що кохання навіки вмерло!

** Пашміна – вид кашмірської шалі, виготовленої з кашемірової вовни, відома ручною вишивкою та м'якістю.*

## Ominous Silence

How can you tell the difference between
a dream and a nightmare?

I woke up to see the war was finally over.
I was relieved and confused.

I did not know who had won.
And how did it all end suddenly?

Did we go nuclear? What else
might have led our world to annihilation?

The angels and the devil were dead.
And God was grieving in heaven.

But you and I were still alive.
Still writing, documenting,

the accounts of the war. You were
transcribing my verses.

But for whom and for what,
when our planet is destroyed?

And those who are alive without eyes and limbs
cannot read and understand what we wrote.

I am astonished! I can still write in the dark,
without ink, pen, and paper, with my broken fingertips,

with blood flowing from my heart,
on the pieces of our precious planet torn apart,

Every warrior who wanted to read love poems is dead.
So, what's the meaning of all that we did together?

What's the meaning of what we are doing now?
What's the meaning of what we want to do next?

Please don't say the answer is in the silence before us.
And our loving hearts—like a bloody battlefield!

## Зловісна тиша

Про відмінність між сном і кошмаром
як розповісти тобі?

Я збудилась, побачити щоб: нарешті війна закінчи́лася.
Я відчула полегкість і розгублення.

Не знала я, хто переміг.
І як це все раптом скінчилося?

Сталось ядерне? Що ж іще
може знищити світ цей?

І диявол, і ангели вмерли.
Бог зажурився на небесах.

Ми ж удвох — ще живі,
у письмі, у фіксації свідчень

і рахунків війни. Ти — присутній,
мої вірші тлумачачи.

Та для кого й для чого,
якщо нашу планету вже знищили?

А всі ті, хто живий, без очей і кінцівок,
прочитати, збагнути не зможуть, що́ ми написали.

Я здивована! Я ще здатна писати у темряві,
без чорнил, без пера, без паперу, пальцями зламаними,

кров'ю, що з серця спливає,
на уламках планети безцінної.

Кожен воїн, який мої вірші любові бажав прочитати,
вже загинув. Тож заради чого все, що разом зробили ми?

Задля чого усе, що ми робимо зараз?
Задля чого усе, що зробити ми схочемо?

Не кажи, я прошу, що у тиші цій — відповідь
і що наші серця — бойовища скривавлені!

## Air Raid: 11:10 - 01.24.23

*"We still have ten minutes to talk, we still have ten minutes*
*to get to the shelter from the time the siren goes off, go on..."*

And I wish I had listened to you.
I wish I could have said something
in those ten minutes, knowing that life is uncertain.
You, too, could have said something to me, knowing
your world was fragile and we may not speak again.

Something could have been done in those ten minutes
to save our world and dreams aborted from our eyes.
We could have found ways to shoot down
the enemy's missiles that struck our hearts to set us apart.
I laugh at my naivety and the cruelty of the world!

But the clock cannot be turned back. I drive around.
Go round and round on the cliff overlooking the Pacific,
where love was shot and drowned. I look at its dark,
murky water-grave from the top, and my saffron scarf of
our California dream goes down. My lips turn cold and purple.

And the full moon—dizzy above my head.

## Сирена повітряної тривоги: 11:10 - 24.01.2023

*«Ми маємо десять хвилин для розмови, десять хвилин від початку тривоги, аби дістатися до укриття, тож продовжуймо...»*

І кортіло мені тебе слухати.
І бажала могти щось сказати
за десяток хвилин цих, непевність життя усвідомлюючи.
Міг і ти щось сказати мені, усвідомлюючи,
що твій світ є крихким — може статися, що спілкуватись не зможемо.

За десяток хвилин цих зробити щось можна було,
щоб спасти наші мрії і світ, що наза́вжди із наших очей
нагло вирвані! Ми могли б відшукати шляхи
позбивати ворожі ракети з їх ударами, щоб розлучити нас…
Я сміюсь над своєю наївністю і жорстокістю світу!

Час назад не вернути. Я ганяю машину по колу.
Ще і ще я обходжу всі скелі під виття океану,
в якому любов потонула, і у водну могилу,
каламутну і темну, вдивляюсь згори, й шарф шафрановий
мрій з Каліфорнії вділ паде. Холодніють, синіють вже губи.

І місяць у повні — аж обертом йде голова.

# I Promise

What did we do to ourselves, my friend?
We drank the water of *Zamzam** yet remained thirsty.

We saw the beauty and essence of *Udumbara*** blooming
in three thousand years before our eyes and pretended to be blind.

We bathed in its scent and breathed in its fragrance. Yet we lie
near death, by denying the rare celestial boons granted to us.

Love shielded us from heaven to earth, then how did
such horrors strike us? *Check, check, check!*

Your defense system might have been compromised! We can't
afford to lose the war we have committed to fighting together.

Our loved ones are already dead, dear *Arjuna.**** See from the
divine eyes. Pick up your weapons and fight for the sake of humanity.

Why were we expelled from heaven if we didn't eat
the forbidden fruit?**** Ask God!

What was He thinking? Where was He when the world
blamed and shamed for the offenses we didn't commit?

Did he delegate His job to the devil, who entered our souls
in disguise, to extinguish the light we carried for each other?

He must have. He is pretentious. But how could He?!!!
I will wait at heaven's gate until He returns.

Until He faces me! Or else there won't be,
any believers left on earth, I promise!

**Zamzam — A sacred well in Mecca, Saudi Arabia, located 20 miles east of the Ka'ba, the holiest place in Islam.*
***Udumbara — A rare celestial flower mentioned in Buddhism which blooms only once, every three thousand years, when Tathagata descend on earth to remove the sufferings of the universe.*
****Arjuna — A warrior prince and the chief protagonist of the Hindu epic Mahabharata.*
*****Genesis 3:7*

## Я обіцяю

Зробили що собі, мій друже?
Замзамську* воду ми пили, не втамуваши спрагу.

Красу і сутність удумбари** , що за три тисячоліття розквітла вперше
перед нами, ми побачили, але прикинулись незрячими.

Ми вмились пахощами і вдихнули аромат. Та перед смертю
від надзвичайних благ, згори нам подарованих, ми відмовляємось.

Кохання захищало нас від неба до землі, тому такі жахіття
як спіткали нас? Спинімось, перевірмо, перевірмо!

Твою систему захисту зламали, вочевидь! Дозволити
війну програти, яку погодились вести разом, ми не повинні.

Кохані наші вже загинули, о дорогий Арджуно*** . Поглянь
священним зором. І візьми свій меч на боротьбу заради людства.

Чому нас скинули із неба, якщо не скуштували плоду
ми забороненого?**** Бога запитай!

Що думав Він? І де Він був у час, коли цей світ
у прогріхах нас звинуватив, яких і не чинили ми?

Чи дияволу дозволив увійти приховано у душі,
аби згасити світло, яке несли навзаєм ми?

Напевно, так. Таж він вимогливий. Але як може Він?!!!
Я перед брамою небесною чекатиму, аж поки Він повернеться,

аж поки ми побачимось! Інакше вже не буде на землі
нікого з тих, хто вірить ще, я обіцяю!

** Замзам — священний колодязь у Мецці, Саудівська Аравія, одне з головних місць хаджу в ісламському світі.*
*** Удумбара — див. примітку до однойменної поезії.*
**** Арджуна — принц-воїн і головний герой індуїстського епосу «Махабхарата». В поезії авторка звертається до дилеми: вести війну на полі битви чи скласти зброю, аби не бачити смерті близьких. Крішна священним зором показав Арджуні, що близькі вже мертві, але їхні душі безсмертні. Боротьба ж дозволить зберегти народ і царство: «Бгаґавад-Ґіта», розділ 2, вірші 31–38.*
**** Буття 3:7.

## Tomb of Love

Among all the casualties of war,
love is a silent death.

You do not hear about
the temples of love razed by warriors.
You never find tombs of love in a war.

Love is not even worth a number,
a grave, a flower, or a eulogy.

In a victory speech, no commander talks about
the loss of love, a defeated cause! No one rallies
and petitions for love in the United Nations.

Love, like a lost cause, is sucked into
the black hole of the sky after being shot in mid-air.

Dear President Volodymyr, I hope
you talk about love someday,
in your victory speech.

And let me know,
where to find the tomb of my love.

# Могила кохання

Між усіх жертв війни
любов — смерть непомітна.
Не говорять ніколи про
храми любові, зруйновані воїнами.
Не знайти на війні і цвинтаря любові.

Любов не вартує ні обліку,
ані могили, ні квітки, ані прощальних присвят.

У переможній промові командир і не скаже про
втрати любові, про розбиті надії! Демонстрацій
не буде, не буде й петицій стосовно любові в ООН.

Любов, наче програна справа, вже засмоктана
у чорну діру, що у небі від пострілів виникла.

Вельмишановний Президенте Володимире,
я сподіваюся: в переможній промові
ти про любов не забудеш.

І дай мені знати,
де поховання любові моєї знайти.

## Udumbara

Love cannot die. Don't be a fool.
No weapon can cut and destroy love.
Don't you try! Don't you cry!

Love survives on its own.
Lovers do not keep love alive.
Love keeps lovers alive.

When you can't see, smell,
touch, or taste, love still exists.
When extinct, it's reborn.

It carves a shape for itself
that cannot be seen,
but it's always there.

Love is a river. When it dies, it becomes a cloud.
The cloud becomes rain and returns to earth.
Love is born every moment, simultaneously with death.

It is being born right now as a teardrop,
about to fall from our eyes as we plan its grand funeral,
and angels and valentines regard us in dismay.

Not every seed of love sees the daylight. Some are born
in the darkest of night. They carry light in their buds.
Some bloom only once in three thousand years, like *Udumbara,* *

which manifests only when
*Tathagatas* ** with virtues descend on earth
to remove the sufferings of the universe.

What bloomed in our hearts and faded was *Udumbara,*
meant to blossom just once in three thousand years!

**Udumbara—A auspicious celestial flower mentioned in Buddhist scriptures that does not exist in the mundane world. It's a supernatural phenomenon.*
***Tathagata (male or female) is the one who comes to us through the right path."*

## Удумбара*

Любов не може вмерти. Не кажи дурниць!
Аби зарізати і знищити любов, немає зброї.
Не прагни навіть! Не кричи!

Любов сама по собі виживає.
Закохані любові не бережуть.
Закоханих любов береже.

Коли й не бачиш, не торкаєшся, не пробуєш
на смак чи запах, все одно любов існує.
Якщо і зникне, то відродиться допевне.

Вона різьбить свою форму,
яку й не видно,
хоч вона існує.

Любов — ріка. Вмираючи, стає хмариною,
яка стає дощем, вертаючись на землю.
Любов з'являється щомиті, зі смертю поруч.

Народжується саме тепер, мов сльоза, щоб упасти
з очей, коли готуємо її величне поховання,
а янголи та валентини із жахом дивляться на нас.

Не все зерно любові бачить світло. Є й народжене
у найтемнішій ночі. Воно в бруньках нестиме світло.
Цвістимуть деякі лиш раз на три тисячоліття, неначе удумбара*,

надземна, що звіщає світові,
коли на землю зійдуть татхагати*,
усунути аби всесвітні муки.

Це удумбара цвіла в серцях, але зів'яла,
що трапилося раз на три тисячоліття!

* *Удумбара — благовісна небесна квітка із буддистських писань, якої не існує у звичному світі. Вона — надприродна.*
** *Татхагата — той, хто приходить до нас правильним шляхом.*

## Nothing is Permanent

And one day, she wrote no poems.
The light extinguished, and the darkness crept in.

She was taken by sailors on a dark ship in deep waters,
where her body was traded with another body.

Uyava wasn't a goddess, just a mythical character.
But her demise is real, and her legends will live on.

She will live as hope lives in your forlorn heart,
from sunrise to sunset, every moment,

not as sharp as a knife blade that cuts through your heart,
but ripe and sweet like a fruit in the sun you cannot reach.

Do not grieve for her, dear Ukraine.
Nothing is permanent, not even love.

## Ніщо не є вічним

І одного дня вона не написала ані вірша.
Світло згасло, і темрява запанувала.

Тримали її матроси на темному кораблі на глибоких водах,
де її тілом торгували разом з іншим тілом.

І Уява була не богинею — мітом,
та кончина — реальна, а легенди про неї — живі,

й буде жити подібно надії в твоєму розбитому серці,
від сходу сонця до заходу, миті кожної,

не гостра, неначе лезо, що крає серце тобі,
а достигла й солодка, мов плід на осонні, якого тобі не зірвати.

За нею не журись, Краю милий — дорога Україно.
Ніщо не є вічним, любов також.

## Knowing

I dipped my toe in a stream
not knowing it was a sea.

## Пізнання

Я занурила пальчик ніженьки у потічок,
а той виявився морем безкраїм.

## Жовто-синя, по-індійськи містична, книга віршів

Любов, Свобода – основні, універсальні духовно-поетичні егрегори, які об'єднують всі народи у всі часи. Нині доля людства вирішується в Україні, тому знаменно, що підполковник героїчних Збройних Сил України, поет Володимир Тимчук, якого особисто знаю і читаю давно, переклав жовто-синю (колір українського прапора), по-індійськи містичну, книгу віршів «Любовні листи до України» чудової індійсько-американської поетеси Калпни Сінг Чітніс, які оце побачили світ як українсько-англійська білінгва в американському видавництві «River Paw Press», співтворячи нову інформаційно-культурну реальність і наближаючи мир як результат перемоги Добра у глобальному земному світі із проекцією на вічність і безкрайність людських душ у багатобарвному та єдиному життєдайному пульсуючому ритмі, де розмаїті струни-стежки, але єдиний і красивий Шлях людства – до Творця.

Нехай ця екзотична і органічна Книга із віршами на кшталт:

*Я за світлом твоїм йшла додому свій шлях, // Та не знаю, звідкіль ця дорога була // І яким є у мене ім'я? Краю милий, // Мене називай вже Уявою! –*

як спільна душевна дитина представників індійського та українського народів на краплину, на іскорку, метафору наблизить усіх нас до катарсису...

*~ Ігор Павлюк, письменник, перекладач і науковець, народний поет України, лауреат Премії британського ПЕН-клубу, лауреат Швейцарської літературної премії 2021 року, доктор наук із соціальних комунікацій.*

## «Любовні листи до України» як зразок інтимної лірики

Любов, яка виникає з образу Вогню і переростає у дуже інтимну, довірливу ноту. Поетка відчуває Україну не просто своєю уявою, а кожним мініметром свого тіла і душі. Тому її почуття, змішані з жахом і гнівом, з кожним новим днем вибухають віршем, який подорожує світом і повертається додому. Це не просто цикл віршів – це спосіб ПІЗНАВАННЯ – через дотики, звуки, кольори, занурюючи кожен пальчик і вимірюючи ним глибину образу, який ховається за мапою, що окреслює фізичні і ментальні простори України.

Думки, які збурюють «зловісну тишу» і «сирени повітряних тривог», вправно виконують свою ритуальну місію, як мантра із буддистських писань. Тому що ці думки несуть особливо благовісну енергію творення, яку метафорично уособлює у циклі віршів небесна квітка Удумбара.
Проживаючи дні жахливого 2022 року із повномасштабним вторгненням в Україну загарбницьких військ росії у дуже конкретних часових образах і просторово впізнаваних локаціях, авторка пише не просто поетичний щоденник воєнного часу, а особливий псалом віри:

*«Я чую слова, не кажеш які ти, // пишу їх у записнику // і слухаю, наче Псалми».*

Відтак, образ Фенікса для неї є найбільш доказовим, переконливим і довірливим способом спілкування з Україною з-поза іншого краю океану:

*Якщо є інший день, якщо є життя інше, // як Фенікс я обіцяю постати // із попелу свого буття // у небі твоїм, синьо-жовтім.*

Патріотичні вірші Калпни Сінг-Чітніс є оригінальною інтерпретацією авторки інтимної лірики, яка виростає на ґрунті ностальгійного вчування в образ України з намаганням вийти за рамки патетики та риторики хрестоматійних уявлень та розширити горизонти образів, розриваючи страхи і давні рани однісіньким словом – ЛЮБОВ.

*~ Маріанна Челецька, літературознавець*

**Volodymyr Tymchuk** is a Ukrainian poet, writer, translator, and lieutenant colonel of the Armed Forces of Ukraine who participates in the Russian-Ukrainian war. He was a senior teacher at the Hetman Petro Sahaidachnyi National Army Academy and is a Candidate in Technical Sciences. Tymchuk, who began his literary career with his debut poetry collection «Vesniani kolovoroty» ("Spring Whirlpools") (2009), has published over a dozen collections of poetry, poetry anthologies and books of prose in the Ukrainian language. His first collection of poems also included his translations from Slavic languages, featuring poems by the President of the Chechen Republic of Ichkeria, Zelimkhan Yandarbiyev. His first collection of short stories and essays, «Slovodiem» ("Word-Acted"), was published in 2014. In 2015, on the anniversary of the deportation of Crimean Tatars by Russia (Soviet "Union" at that time) commemorated the victims of the deportation to remind the world that occupiers and their collaborators were still committing crimes against humanity in the annexed Autonomous Republic of Crimea and the city of Sevastopol, and the idea of the art project «Bakhchysarai. 2021» was born in the city of Lviv. Volodymyr Tymchuk and authors like S. Kokche, Maye Safet, six translators, and four artists prepared a unique edition of the first bilingual book written in the Ukrainian and Crimean Tatar languages in three months, which was presented with a question "Do we, the authors, expect a presentation in the liberated Ukrainian Bakhchysarai in six years?" He also authored «To Burn and Fire, to Outlive and Overcome!» (2016), the first collection of war poems. In 2017 Tymchuk created another significant project called «Ukraine and Lithuania: At the Crossroads of Histories and Values» based on the postcards by Vidmantas Kudarauskas from Lithuania and First Day Covers from *Ukrposhta* and *Lietuvos paštas* for the parallel placement and comparisons of the historical events of two ancient European nations who valued freedom in their expressions. He edited «Verlaine and the Song» (2017), an anthology with one French poem and 40 versions of its Ukrainian poetic interpretations, and «Opus Khody. № 2399» ("March Opus") (2018) with his Lithuanian friend Juozas Valiušaitis in just 69 hours and 21 minutes, which was challenged to the Guinness Book of World Records for creating the fastest book from concept to completion. Between 2018 and 2022, he worked on writing, translating, editing, and publishing several literary projects, such as the translations of war poems of the 1st World war poets from English, German, Hungarian; the translations of Christmas poems from Byelorussian, Latvian, Italian, Portugal, and other cultures, and the key anthology «In principio erat Verbum: Ukrainian poems of war» about first 100 days of Life from February 24, 2022, in Ukrainian and French. During this period, he also authored: «The B.a:S-i)l's #light» (2018) «Vidchuty misto stopoyu (z Toboyu» (2019), «In Angels' Order» (2019), «East … Sunrise» (2020), «Azov Crossed» (2020), «From Cossack Hetmanate's infinity» (2021). His awards and honors include the "Bohdan Khmelnytskyi Prize" for the best coverage of military themes in literature and art (2016), the "Markiyan Shashkevych Poetic Nomination for Lviv Regional Cultural Prize" (2020), and "Volyanik-Shwabinskyi Literary and Scientific Award" (2022). He is the translator of "Love Letters to Ukraine from Uyava" (2023) by Kalpna Singh-Chitnis, forthcoming from River Paw Press, and working on his next poetry collection, «Те слово, що зцілює» ("Ukraine: The Healing Word") Website: www.volodymyrtymchuk.wordpress.com

**Kalpna Singh-Chitnis** is an Indian-American poet, writer, filmmaker, and author of six poetry collections. Her works have appeared in notable journals such as *"World Literature Today," "Columbia Journal," "Tupelo Quarterly," "Indian Literature," "Vsesvit," "Silk Routes Project"* (IWP) at The University of Iowa, Stanford University's *"Life in Quarantine,"* etc. Poems from her award-winning book *Bare Soul* and her poetry film "River of Songs" have been included in the "Nova Collection" and the "Polaris Collection" of the Lunar Codex time capsules going on the Moon with NASA's Nova-C lander missions to Oceanus Procellarum and "NASA VIPER" rover mission to the Lunar South Pole in 2023. Her poems "The Tree" and "Coming Home" (Bare Soul) have been included in college and university curricula in India and in the UK.

Her latest collection of poems, "Love Letters to Ukraine from Uyava," River Paw Press (2023), dedicated to Ukraine and its defenders, has been translated into Ukrainian by poet and translator Volodomyr Tymchuk, a lieutenant colonel of the Armed Forces of Ukraine.

Kalpna's poetry has received praise from eminent writers, such as Nobel Prize in Literature nominee Dr. Wazir Agha, Vaptsarov Award, and Ordre des Arts et des Lettres recipient Amrita Pritam, and poet and Academy Award winning lyricist and filmmaker Gulzar. She has read at the International Literature Festival Berlin (ilb), Sahitya Akademi, India's highest academy of letters, Poets & Writers, AWP Conferences, and other venues internationally. Her works have been translated into fifteen languages and published in anthologies worldwide. The most recent among them are *100 Great Indian Poems* (Bloomsbury, India), *Unseen* (Skylark Publications, UK), *Collateral Damage, Carrying the Branch Poets in Search of Peace* (Glass Lyre Press, USA), *The Kali Project* (Indie Blu(e) Publishing), *Paws Healing the Earth, Oxygen: Parables of the Pandemic,* and *Sunflowers: Ukrainian Poetry on War Resistance Hope and Peace* (River Paw Press).

As a filmmaker, Kalpna Singh-Chitnis is known for writing and directing her debut feature, "Goodbye My Friend" (2011). She won the "Silver Award" for writing, directing, and producing "Girl With An Accent" (short) at SMTV Mumbai International Film Festival. "Girl With An Accent" Television Premiered on LA18 TV in California and Hawaii on May 26, 2015. Her environmental film "The Tree " (2022), based on her work of poetry, has won several awards at international film festivals, including the "Best Experimental Short Film Award" at the North Dakota Environmental Rights Film Festival.

She has been nominated for a pushcart prize, and her awards and honors include the 2017 "Naji Naaman Literary Prize for Creativity," the "Bihar Rajbhasha Award," given by the government of Bihar, India, "Bihar Shri," and the "Rajiv Gandhi Global Excellence Award." A former lecturer of Political Science and the Editor-in-Chief of *Life and Legends*, Kalpna Singh-Chitnis is the Translation Editor of *IHRAF WRITES*, and an Advocacy Member of the United Nations Association of the USA. She holds a degree in Film Directing from the NYFA and works as an independent filmmaker in Hollywood. Her latest poetry collection *Trespassing My Ancestral Lands* is forthcoming from Finishing Line Press. Website: www.kalpnasinghchitnis.com